Praise for *Fast 5K* and Pete Magill

"Pete Magill's running career has shown he's the 'master of the 5K.' This guidebook proves that he's also the best at teaching others how to improve their 5K performance. Do what Pete says, and you're sure to run stronger, healthier, and faster."

—AMBY BURFOOT, 1968 Boston Marathon winner and author of
Run Forever and *The Runner's Guide to the Meaning of Life*

"If you want to run a faster 5K but don't know where to start, Pete Magill has done the research so you don't have to. In *Fast 5K*, he combines years of experience as a coach and competitor with the latest science to help you get the most out of your training. He's truly a 5K runner's best friend."

—CLAUDETTE GROENENDAAL, USA National Champion, NCAA Champion,
former NCAA Women's national record holder for 800 meters

"I've said it before, and I'm saying it again: If you want to run faster, do what Pete Magill says. It's that simple."

—SCOTT DOUGLAS, *Runner's World* contributing writer and author of
Advanced Marathoning and *The Athlete's Guide to CBD*

"Pete's latest marvel of scholarship is a hoot to read and a treasure to follow. Pete explodes all ignorance while sharing the most intelligent steps to 5K excellence."

—KEN STONE, founder and editor of *Masterstrack.blog*,
contributing editor for *Times of San Diego*

"Pete Magill's *Fast 5K* is like having a personal coach at your fingertips. His easy-to-digest keys break down the components of 5K training in a way that will benefit runners of all abilities. You'll want to read this book before you start training for your next 5K—or you might get beat by someone who did."

—SEAN WADE, Olympic marathoner, masters world record holder,
and founder of the Kenyan Way

"Pete Magill is the Mr. Miyagi of running. He will build you up comprehensively for a lifetime of happy running, and you won't even have to paint his fence or wax his car."

—JAY DUPLASS, American film director, author, and actor

"This thorough book covers all aspects of training and racing the 5K, yet reads with an easy familiarity, based on Magill's experience as a runner, coach, and student of the sport. Magill knows what you need to do to improve and where you're likely to make mistakes. Anyone who reads and follows this book will undoubtably become a better runner and likely end up with a 5K PR."

—JONATHAN BEVERLY, editor-in-chief of *PodiumRunner*, and author of *Run Strong, Stay Hungry* and *Your Best Stride*

"Whether you're just starting out as a runner or starting afresh, you can do no better than heed the guidance of running's ultimate comeback kid, Pete Magill."

—MATT FITZGERALD, author of *How Bad Do You Want It?* and *Racing Weight*

"Pete Magill must have found the fountain of youth. I coach college students, and he consistently outruns half my team! He must know something the rest of us don't!"

—STEVE SCOTT, head track coach at Cal State San Marcos, 3-time Olympian, former American record holder in the mile

FAST
5K

FAST

25 CRUCIAL KEYS AND **4** TRAINING PLANS

5K

PETE MAGILL

Boulder, Colorado

4745 Walnut Street, Suite 100
Boulder, CO 80301–2651 USA

VeloPress is the leading publisher of books on endurance sports and is a division of Pocket Outdoor Media. Focused on cycling, triathlon, running, swimming, and nutrition/diet, VeloPress books help athletes achieve their goals of going faster and farther. Preview books and contact us at velopress.com.

Distributed in the United States and Canada by Ingram Publisher Services

A Cataloging-in-Publication record for this book is available from the Library of Congress.

ISBN 978-1-937715-92-2

This paper meets the requirements of ANSI/NISO Z39.48-1992 (Permanence of Paper).

Art direction by Vicki Hopewell
Design by Graham Smith
Composition by Anita Koury

19   20   21 / 10   9   8   7   6   5   4   3   2   1

Contents

PART THREE **RACE-DAY KEYS**

PART FOUR **WORKOUTS & TRAINING PLANS**

Introduction

A Fast 5K

So you want to run a fast 5K.

But you're not sure how to train for it—or, once trained, how to execute the perfect race.

Relax. You're not alone. Every year, between nine and ten million Americans run a 5K race. Some are happy just to finish. But others, like you, want more.

You want to run faster. Faster than you've run recently, faster than you have in your current age group, or maybe faster than ever before.

And you suspect that if you could gain access to the training and racing secrets that allow elite runners to log stellar race after stellar race, you, too, could unlock the magic of your own 5K performance.

The good news is that you're right: There are training, lifestyle, and race adjustments that will make you a better and faster 5K runner.

The bad news is that there is no magic bullet—no single adjustment that on its own will net you the performance you're after.

There's a Bateke proverb that goes like this: "The river swells with the contribution of the small streams." You'll need to create your own "river" by embracing a wide variety of key practices. That's because the 5K is a unique race that pairs the speed of a miler with the endurance of a marathoner. Only a multifaceted approach—one that targets both speed and endurance fitness—will yield your faster 5K.

Sound like a lot to put on your plate?

Again, relax. Training for a faster 5K has more to do with variety, fun, and self-confidence than it does with pain, discipline, and sacrifice. The trick is making sure that your training and lifestyle adjustments provide the keys for unlocking your 5K potential. That's what this book is all about.

PART ONE

TRAINING
KEYS

Set a Reasonable Goal

On the surface, this key seems simple: Set a 5K performance goal that is manageable.

Yet this is where many runners make their first mistake.

A 25-minute 5K runner sets a goal of 22 minutes. Or an 18:30 runner targets 16:45. Or another runner wants to somehow get faster in the four weeks before a local 5K.

All these runners have one thing in common: They're setting a benchmark for success that is difficult, if not impossible, to achieve within a reasonable training time frame. Often, the result will be a negative 5K race experience.

A smarter performance goal is this: Run faster for your next 5K than you did for your last one, and then continue to improve after that. At this stage, don't target an actual time; instead, be satisfied with improved fitness and whatever time improvement that fitness yields. (You can target a specific time in Key 12.)

This isn't about embracing a Zen approach to the sport. It's about recognizing two important concepts that guide successful 5K training programs:

1 Improvement is always incremental (and occurs at different rates for different runners), making it counterproductive to train harder than necessary to achieve incremental gains in performance.

2 Targeting a performance that can't be achieved at your next 5K robs you of the positive feedback you'll experience from targeting a more modest performance goal that's within reach. Don't create a negative environment in which smaller, incremental improvements are viewed as undeserving of celebration—or, worse yet, as failures.

This isn't to imply that you shouldn't have long-term performance goals—including time-specific goals. Many high school, college, and open runners target qualifying times for conference, regional, and national competitions. Masters (age 40+) runners often want to match (or beat) times they ran as younger athletes. And a specific goal time is easier to focus on than the more abstract concept of incremental improvement. It's just that your primary goal should be to institute the type of training, lifestyle, and race execution changes—represented by the keys in this book—that will build the strongest physical version of your running body and remold your mental approach to competition.

Besides, as your training takes hold and you begin to improve, you just might discover that your original long-term 5K goal—rather than being too optimistic—falls short of your true potential. You might end up running faster than you thought possible.

"It's not the will to win that matters—everyone has that. It's the will to prepare to win that matters."

—Paul "Bear" Bryant, six-time national championship football coach at the University of Alabama

Climbing the Steps to 5K Success

COMPONENTS ▶ STEPS

Race	**5K RACE**
Sharpening	Pace work and tune-ups.
Patience	One incremental step at a time.
Consistency	Don't skip workouts. Don't sabotage recovery.
Lifestyle adjustments	Eat, sleep, and recover. Balance running and non-running activities.
Mental training	Perform each workout at the correct effort. Focus on the task at hand.
Physical training	Strengthen your heart, muscles, connective tissue, nervous system, and energy systems.

The key to successful 5K training isn't setting overly ambitious time-related race goals. It's implementing effective training, lifestyle, and race-day strategies—patiently, incrementally, one step at a time.

Schedule a Sensible Training Volume & Intensity

KEY

"If I had five minutes to chop down a tree, I'd spend the first three sharpening my axe." —Anonymous woodsman

Distance-running legend Gerry Lindgren, considered one of the greatest American high school distance runners of all time, regularly logged 150 to 200 running miles per week. And Lindgren claimed, in a 2011 *Runner's World* interview, that "on the weekends when I didn't have anything to do, I'd get up early in the morning and take a sack lunch and run the whole day. I'd sometimes get 100 miles a day during a weekend." At the opposite end of the spectrum, the USA's only Olympic gold medalist at 5000 meters, Bob Schul, trained all high-quality intervals. Schul's morning workout consisted of repetitions at 100, 150, and 200 meters, and his afternoon sessions included repetitions from 100 to 400 meters. His Sunday workout was twenty 400-meter repetitions, with the pace of each rep ranging from 54 to 60 seconds.

Lindgren was all about volume (i.e., overall mileage).

Schul prized intensity (i.e., hard effort).

Both were incredibly successful—and you won't want to follow either's example.

Instead, adopt the Goldilocks approach: When it comes to volume and intensity, you don't want too much, and you don't want too little; you want a balance of both that's "just right" for you.

So how do you determine what's right for you?

First, don't rely on generic prescriptions for volume and intensity. There is no universal guideline for volume that works for all runners. There is no breakdown of workout intensity—no percentage of hard running versus easy running, no absolute total volume of work to be done at more intense paces, no rigid cycle of hard and easy days—that is appropriate across all ages, abilities, body types, levels of experience, and number of workout days per week.

Instead, you'll need to fall back on one of the oldest tricks in the training book: trial and error. Using trial and error, you'll aim to land on a volume and intensity that:

▸ Your body can handle without incurring injury or excessive fatigue
▸ Targets all the physiological and psychological requirements of the 5K
▸ Includes only incremental, periodic increases in volume and intensity as you progress in your program—this can vary from as little as a 10 percent increase for runners who begin their program at high volume/intensity to as much as 50 percent or more for runners who start at a very low volume/intensity

Experienced runners should begin any new 5K training program with a volume and an intensity that are similar to their current levels. Beginners should start with a minimal training stimulus (e.g., walking). From there, you'll incrementally increase volume and intensity. To guide this increase, there are two rules that are popular with runners.

The best-known rule is the 10 Percent Rule. This rule recommends increasing volume at a rate of 10 percent per week, and it promises improved fitness with minimal injury risk. The problem with the 10 Percent Rule is that it's too conservative for beginning runners and too

3-Week Rule vs. 10% Rule for Increasing Volume (mileage)								
WEEK 1 VOLUME	5 MILES/ WEEK		10 MILES/ WEEK		30 MILES/ WEEK		50 MILES/ WEEK	
Week	3-week	10%	3-week	10%	3-week	10%	3-week	10%
1	5	5.0	10	10.0	30	30.0	50	50.0
2	5	5.5	10	11.0	30	33.0	50	55.0
3	5	6.1	10	12.1	30	36.3	50	60.5
4	12	6.7	17	13.3	37	39.9	58	66.6
5	12	7.3	17	14.6	37	43.9	58	73.2
6	12	8.1	17	16.1	37	48.3	58	80.5
7	18	8.9	23	17.7	43	53.1	67	88.6
8	18	9.7	23	19.5	43	58.5	67	97.4
9	18	10.7	23	21.4	43	64.3	67	107.2
10	25	11.8	30	23.6	50	70.7	75	117.9
11	25	13.0	30	25.9	50	77.8	75	129.7
12	25	14.3	30	28.5	50	85.6	75	142.7

For low-volume runners, the 10% Rule creates mileage increases that are well below the body's ability to adapt. For higher volume runners, the 10% Rule leads to increases that are likely to produce injury or burnout. The 3-Week Rule is more physiologically sound.

aggressive for experienced runners—plus, a 2007 study of more than 500 runners found identical injury rates between those following the 10 Percent Rule and those scheduling more rapid increases.

A better approach is the Three-Week Rule. After each jump in volume and intensity, you give your body three weeks to adapt before scheduling another major increase. This allows you to schedule regular, balanced increases in volume and intensity with a decreased risk of injury. There are several reasons why this is true:

- ▸ While muscles can handle weekly increases in training, connective tissue can't—you end up with injuries such as Achilles tendinitis, shin splits, and stress fractures. By limiting major increases to every third week, you allow connective tissue time to adapt.
- ▸ You exert more control over your program—you pick your eventual goal workload, then distribute increases evenly to achieve that goal.
- ▸ You decrease both physical and mental stress by allowing your body to adapt to a workload before increasing it.

Eventually, you'll discard the Three-Week Rule and schedule increases using the method famously put forward by the late Dr. George Sheehan: "Listen to your body."

Train All Your
5K Running Muscles

We humans have almost 700 different muscles. When you run a 5K, you use most of them.

Unfortunately, if you're like most runners, you've failed to train most of the muscles—specifically, the muscle fibers—that you'll use during a 5K. This common training lapse can be attributed to two related misconceptions:

1   The belief that individual muscles (e.g., your hamstrings or biceps) are single units in which all muscle fibers are turned "on" or "off" as one—for example, the belief that all the muscle fibers in your calf muscle contract if you go up on your tippy toes.
2   The belief that all running workouts train all muscle fibers within a working muscle—it's just that some workouts train fibers more intensely than others (e.g., thinking a distance run trains all the muscle fibers in your leg muscles, just less intensely than 400-meter reps at 5K pace).

Reality check: Your running muscles do not function as single units; each muscle uses only as many of its muscle fibers as is required to perform an activity.

In fact, you use only a small percentage of the muscle fibers in your leg muscles for low-key exercises, such as walking. Similarly, distance runs recruit far fewer muscle fibers than you'll use running a 5K—and almost none of the fibers you'll need to run that 5K fast.

Each one of your muscles is composed of three types of muscle fibers:

- ▶ Slow-twitch
- ▶ Intermediate fast-twitch (we'll just call these "intermediate" from now on)
- ▶ Fast-twitch

When you exercise, these fibers are recruited in a "ladder." The first rung of the ladder is slow-twitch. You use almost exclusively slow-twitch fibers for low-intensity work, such as walking and jogging. As the intensity of your activity increases (e.g., you pick up your pace during a run, accelerating from jogging to a less-conversational effort), you move up a rung in the ladder, adding intermediate fibers, which produce more power and contract more quickly than slow-twitch fibers. If your intensity increases even more (e.g., you run up a steep hill or sprint to the 5K finish line), you add fast-twitch fibers to the mix, which are even bigger cells and contract fastest and most powerfully of all. When you're simultaneously using all three muscle-fiber types, you've reached the top rung of the ladder.

The chart, Muscle Fiber Types Used at Various Paces, illustrates the percentage of each fiber type that's required to maintain different paces. (Keep in mind that real-world fiber recruitment will vary from person to person.) From the chart, you can see that running a fast 5K requires training a lot of muscle fibers. I've had runners complain to me after a 5K, "Wow, I'm really sore!" They're sore because they trained

"The strength of the team is each individual member. The strength of each member is the team." —Phil Jackson, 11-time NBA championship coach

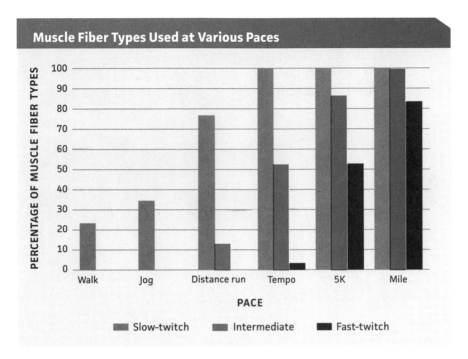

Muscle Fiber Types Used at Various Paces

At different paces, you recruit different percentages of your muscle fibers. 5K race pace recruits all slow-twitch fibers, most intermediate fibers, and more than 50 percent of fast-twitch fibers.

only slow-twitch fibers in preparation for the race (e.g., they stuck to an all-distance diet) and toed the start line with untrained intermediate and fast-twitch fibers. Those faster fibers simply weren't ready to race.

Let's say a farmer wants to plant his field. First, he plows it. Next, he plants seeds. Finally, he waters a third of the field. On the next day, he waters the same third of the field. And on the next, the same third. This goes on every day, the farmer watering the same third of the field. After a month, crops are only growing on the third of the field the farmer has watered. He can't figure out what's gone wrong. *Hey, dummy, you only watered a third of your field!* Don't be a dummy. Water your entire field.

To train each muscle-fiber type for maximum performance, you'll need to schedule a variety of workouts. We'll discuss specific workouts that allow you to target your full range of fibers in Keys 4 through 15. For now, understand that a major key to 5K preparation is training all the muscle fibers you'll use to achieve your best performance.

Slow Down Your Distance Runs

"Good things come slow, especially in distance running."

—Bill Dellinger, Olympian and five-time NCAA championship coach

Distance runs are the primary way you train slow-twitch muscle fibers.

Most runners understand that it's the cumulative volume of distance runs that provides the foundation for success as a distance runner. That's true whether you're training for a 5K or a marathon. That said, runners make a mistake when they assume that up-tempo distance runs are more effective than runs performed at a comfortable effort level. In fact, many runners sabotage their training by doing their distance runs too hard.

First, let's dispel a running myth: Running your distance runs slowly won't make you a slow runner. Training incorrectly—not doing the full range of workouts required to build speed—will make you a slow runner.

The correct pace for your distance runs is the pace that guarantees you'll get 100 percent of the benefits you're hoping to reap from those runs. So step one (as with any workout) is to determine those targeted benefits. For distance runs, the training adaptations you're after include:

▸ Strengthening slow-twitch muscle fibers
▸ Strengthening connective tissue like bones and tendons
▸ Increasing the number and size of mitochondria (microscopic, aerobic energy–producing power plants) within each slow-twitch fiber

- Increasing the number of capillaries surrounding each slow-twitch fiber (capillaries are tiny blood vessels that carry oxygen and nutrients to your muscle fibers)
- Increasing the amount of carbohydrate fuel (i.e., glycogen) stored within each slow-twitch fiber
- Strengthening your heart, so that you can pump more blood with each heartbeat
- Improving your nervous system's ability to recruit slow-twitch fiber into action, thereby creating a more efficient stride and reducing the amount of energy you'll expend

To trigger all these adaptations, you need to run at about 65–75 percent VO_2max. In layman's terms, that means running at a conversational pace—about two minutes per mile slower than 5K pace for faster runners, and up to three minutes per mile for slower runners. At that effort level, your body receives the correct stimulus. Equally important, you'll recover in time for the next day's workout. Run harder than that, and you recruit faster fibers, creating nervous-system fatigue and increasing your use of anaerobic energy, both of which lengthen the time you'll need for recovery. See the Training Paces table (p. 128) for pacing guidelines.

If you're still having trouble keeping your foot off the accelerator, try leaving your watch at home. If you know how far a run is, you don't need to time it. Going watchless removes the temptation to speed up and allows you to settle into a pace that's appropriate for the day—one that matches your fatigue level, the temperature, that stiff lower back from sitting at a desk for eight hours, or some other variable that might affect your pace on that specific day.

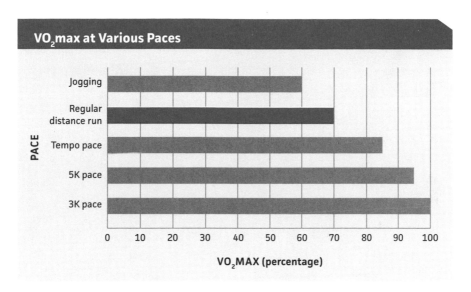

At 70 percent VO_2max, distance runs work a large percentage of slow-twitch fibers, while recruiting only a small percentage of intermediate fibers and almost no fast-twitch fibers. As you increase your pace, your VO_2max also increases, leading to recruitment of faster fibers, increased nervous- and energy-system fatigue, and longer post-run recovery.

My own watchless running began in my mid-40s. I'd been doing the same recovery run for years, and my time had gradually slipped from 45 minutes to 50 minutes. It was depressing. I decided, *Enough!* and left the watch at home the next time I did that run. At the end of the run, my son Sean admitted he'd timed me. "You ran 62 minutes," he said. Turned out, I'd been running too fast all along. After that day, I stopped wearing a watch for distance runs. I slowed my pace. Recovered better. Was stronger on hard days. And saw my race times drop.

Distance runs will make up the bulk of your training volume. And long-term improvement is largely dictated by the accumulation of these runs. But the emphasis is on "long-term." We're talking months and years, not days and weeks.

In the meantime, running distance faster than necessary won't short-cut the process or earn you a faster 5K. Instead, it will leave you tired, heavy-legged, unprepared for the next day's workout, and slower on race day.

Split Tempo Runs into Repetitions

Tempo is quite possibly the most misunderstood workout in running.

And for good reason: Tempo runs can be completed at three different paces, and each of these paces requires a different duration for the workout to be effective. So step one in designing a tempo workout is understanding what paces are considered "tempo":

Marathon pace: a pace you could maintain for a marathon, roughly 40–60 seconds slower than 5K pace; workout calls for 25–30 minutes at this pace

Half-marathon pace: a pace you could maintain for a half-marathon, roughly 25–40 seconds slower than 5K pace; workout calls for 20–25 minutes at this pace

60-minute pace: a pace you could maintain for 60 minutes, roughly 15–25 seconds slower than 5K pace; workout calls for 15–20 minutes at this pace

And then there's the (incorrect) pace at which many runners do their tempo workout: all out.

Let's start with this last approach—tempo run as de facto time trial. Simply put, don't do it. As far as your body is concerned, it's a race, and a race requires a taper beforehand and a few recovery days afterward. It's too hard an effort for a workout.

Next, let's look at the three legitimate tempo paces. All actively engage 100 percent of your available slow-twitch muscle fibers and about 50 percent of available intermediate fibers (more for 60-minute pace, less for marathon pace), stimulating the following adaptations:

- Increased mitochondria for recruited slow-twitch and intermediate fibers
- Increased capillaries for recruited fibers—increasing their supply of nutrients and oxygen
- Improved ability to utilize and clear lactate (a carbohydrate energy source) from within recruited muscle fibers
- Improved ability to buffer and export acidic hydrogen ions from recruited fibers, as well as to manage other fatigue-inducing by-products of anaerobic energy production
- Improved ability to burn fat as a fuel source

So which pace should you choose for your tempo runs? You'll develop better running efficiency for the 5K at paces that are closer to 5K goal race pace, so go with the half-marathon and 60-minute tempo paces.

Which brings us to the key point. Even though tempo should be run at what Olympic coach and author Jack Daniels has defined as "comfortably hard," it's still a workout that results in significant muscular, connective tissue, and nervous-system fatigue. Mistakes in pace judgment (e.g., you choose a 60-minute pace that is faster than what your body is ready to run that day) can lead to system overload. Consequently, it makes sense to break your tempo runs into 5-minute or 10-minute repetitions, with a 2–3-minute jogging recovery interval. Not only does your nervous system get a break, you also have time during the recovery interval to reassess your pace. If you're going too fast (if your effort level exceeds what you could maintain for the targeted half-marathon or 60-minute pace, or if you start breathing as hard as you would during 5K/10K-pace repetitions or a race), then you can slow down during the next repetition.

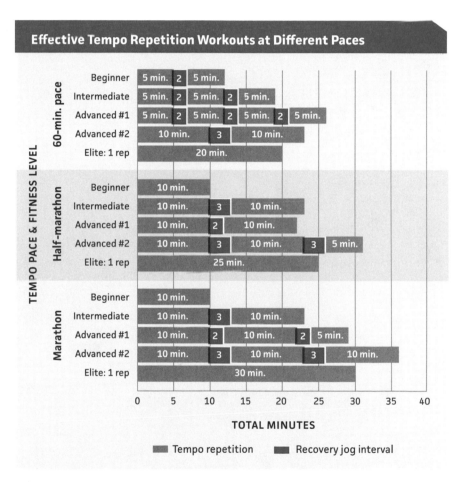

Effective Tempo Repetition Workouts at Different Paces

Most 5K runners choose to run tempo repeats at 60-min. pace or half-marathon pace. Depending on fitness level, you can break your tempo workout into multiple reps, separated by brief jogging recovery intervals.

Note: Advanced includes two options.

Most 5K runners should schedule 2–3 tempo workouts per month. While elite marathoners set aside 15–20 percent of their training for tempo, you'll require a wider range of pace work to generate the fitness arsenal required for a 5K race—it's unlikely you'll have enough available time or energy to perform that much tempo.

"We are what we repeatedly do. Excellence, then, is not an act, but a habit."

—Will Durant, American historian, writer, and philosopher

Include VO$_2$max Workouts

The 5K burns a lot of oxygen.

Improving your 5K performance will require burning even more oxygen. That's because the 5K is 90–95 percent fueled by aerobic energy— energy created within muscle fibers using carbohydrates, fats, and oxygen. When your aerobic energy supply is low, you run slowly. If you can increase the supply, you run faster. You should already have the carbohydrates (see Key 16) and fats you need to produce more aerobic energy. It's oxygen that's deficient. Increase both the oxygen supply and your ability to utilize that supply, and you increase energy production. Increase energy production—and fast 5K, here you come.

You don't increase your oxygen supply by breathing in more air. You increase it by improving transportation of oxygen to your muscle fibers. While your heart and major blood vessels handle bulk transport of oxygen throughout your body, it's the very smallest blood vessels, your capillaries, that deliver oxygen to muscle fibers themselves. Capillaries are so small that red blood cells, which carry oxygen, pass through them in single file. The only way to route more oxygen to a muscle fiber is to create more capillaries. Once delivered, oxygen is used by each muscle fiber's mitochondrial power plants to create energy. The only way to increase energy production is to create more and bigger mitochondria. Bottom line: You need to create more capillaries and bigger, more numerous mitochondria. Otherwise, breathing in more oxygen is like pumping 20 gallons of gas into your car's 10-gallon tank—lots of spillage, but no increase in available fuel.

Distance runs and tempo workouts are effective for increasing the number of capillaries and mitochondria in slow-twitch fibers and some intermediate fibers. But to maximize this adaptation and to extend it to all your intermediate fibers—the key to your 5K performance, because intermediate fibers produce more force and contract more quickly than slow-twitch fibers—you'll need to schedule VO_2max workouts. Your VO_2max is defined as the maximum amount of oxygen that your body can consume in one minute. Again, it's not the amount of oxygen you can breathe into your lungs that counts. It's the amount of oxygen that your mitochondria consume to create energy.

For a VO_2max workout to be effective (i.e., to stimulate the creation of lots of capillaries and mitochondria), you'll need to run repetitions at a minimum of 90 percent of your current VO_2max. Less won't stimulate the improvement you're after; conversely, working at greater than VO_2max will leave you more fatigued without offering an increased benefit. For this reason, runners looking to increase VO_2max train at one of three paces:

▸ **10K pace:** approximately 90 percent VO_2max
▸ **5K pace:** approximately 95 percent VO_2max
▸ **3K pace:** approximately 100 percent VO_2max

For most runners, 5K pace is the best training option. At 5K pace, you get close to maximum benefit without risking the excessive fatigue that can accompany 3K pace, and you're also assured of staying above the 90 percent threshold—a concern for slower runners who use a smaller percentage of VO_2max at 10K pace. On the other hand, super-fit runners who race often—and for whom rep sessions at 5K pace might be too intense an additional workload—often fare better at 10K pace.

VO$_2$max Workouts Progression			
Workout	Number of reps	Length of reps	Recovery interval	Total min. at VO$_2$max
1	6–8	1 min.	1–2 min.	0
2	8	2 min.	2–3 min.	0
3	6	3 min.	3 min.	6
4	4	4 min.	3 min.	8
5	5	4 min.	3 min.	10
6	4	5 min.	3–4 min.	12
7*	4–6	3–6 min.	3–4 min.	12–16

This sample progression of VO$_2$max workouts is best performed during the base-training period. Note that the first workouts include reps that won't produce minutes at VO$_2$max but are essential for building muscle and connective tissue strength. Schedule one VO$_2$max workout per week *or* alternate this progression of VO$_2$max workouts with tempo runs on a weekly basis.

Pick a combination of reps (# of reps and length of reps) that results in 12–16 min. at VO$_2$max; remember that the first 2 min. of any rep don't count toward this total.

(Note: If you don't know your 3K, 5K, or 10K pace, see the Training Paces table on p. 128 for help estimating your pace using your times at race distances from 1500 meters to the half-marathon.)

VO$_2$max reps are best measured in minutes, not distance (e.g., a mile repeat), because it's the amount of time at near-VO$_2$max that counts, not the distance you travel at that effort. For this reason, it's a good idea to do these reps on roads or trails, where you'll find less temptation to compete against yourself—to see if you can go farther by running faster on successive reps—as sometimes happens on a track or measured course.

"If you stay in your comfort zone, you're not going to do anything special."

—Deena Kastor, Olympian and multiple American record holder

VO_2max repetitions should last a minimum of two minutes (it takes approximately two minutes of running for your aerobic system to reach VO_2max), with a maximum length of 6 minutes (4–5 minutes at 3K pace). The recovery interval should be 2–4 minutes.

An exception to the minimum-2-minute repetition rule occurs when shorter reps are combined with 30–40 seconds of recovery. Since VO_2max remains high for 30–40 seconds post-repetition, runners who begin their next rep in that time frame remain at an effective training level—that said, the reps themselves must be short (e.g., 200–400 meters) to avoid excessive fatigue. We'll look at workouts like this in Key 12.

A typical once-per-week progression of VO_2max workouts is illustrated in the VO_2max Workouts Progression table. While some runners will opt to perform this progression in the minimum 6–7 weeks required, with a goal of racing in the near future, other runners will choose to extend their base-training period for 2–3 months before their first important race. The latter group of runners often alternates VO_2max and tempo workouts—either on a weekly basis or with tempo replacing VO_2max training every third or fourth week—as they build more slowly, targeting a larger overall gain in fitness.

Schedule Short Repetitions/Intervals

Running short, fast repetitions (reps) strengthens your heart, sharpens your anaerobic system, and improves leg speed.

Short reps strengthen your heart by increasing your "stroke volume," the amount of blood your heart pumps with each beat. The more blood per beat, the more oxygen you send by way of your bloodstream to your muscles.

Short repetition training, better known as "interval training," dates to the 1930s, when German coach Woldemar Gerschler, influenced by cardiologist Hans Reindell, created the workout. He had athletes run short, intense reps of 100 to 400 meters—however long it took to raise their heart rates to 180 beats per minute. At that point, his athletes immediately slowed to a walk or jog (the recovery "interval"). When their heart rates dropped to 120 beats per minute, they'd start the next rep. If a runner's heart rate took longer than 90 seconds to slow to 120 beats, the workout was finished.

Contrary to what you might think, the workout stimulus occurs during the recovery interval, not the rep. During the recovery interval, returning blood creates a momentary increase in pressure within your heart. This happens because your heart rate (a measure of the blood being pumped away from your heart) drops more quickly than the rate at which previously pumped blood returns to your heart—this stretches your heart chambers, which adapt by increasing in size, which in turn leads to an increase in stroke volume.

"It's true that speed kills. In distance running, it kills anyone who does not have it." —Brooks Johnson, USA Olympic coach

Short reps also build your anaerobic system—the system that provides most of your energy for the first 150–250 meters of a 5K race. When you accelerate off the start line, your energy requirements increase immediately. Your aerobic system can't increase its energy output as quickly. That's because you can't increase aerobic energy production until your lungs, heart, and bloodstream deliver a larger supply of oxygen to your muscles, a process that takes 30–40 seconds. Until then, you rely on anaerobic energy (energy produced within your muscles without using oxygen) to pick up the energy slack. Short reps combined with longer recovery intervals allow you to practice this 30–40-second

Short Repetition Workouts

Pace/ effort level	Fitness level	Number of reps	Length of reps	Recovery interval
1500/mile	Beginner	8–10	30 sec.	60 sec.
	Intermediate	10–15	30 sec.	60 sec.
	Advanced	15–20	30 sec.	60 sec.
3K	Beginner	10–15	30 sec.	60 sec.
	Intermediate (2 options)	15–30	30 sec.	60 sec.
		10–15	45 sec.	75 sec.
	Advanced	8–15	60 sec.	60–90 sec.
Hill repeats	*See Workout Progression for Hill Repeats in Key 9*			

Short reps can be performed at 1500/mile effort or 3K effort. If the listed recovery interval isn't enough to significantly lower your heart rate between reps, it's OK to lengthen your recovery (up to a maximum of 90 sec.). The workout can be performed on roads, trails, grass, or track.

anaerobic energy burn multiple times (note that short recovery intervals are counterproductive, as they allow your aerobic energy system to remain powered up, negating the need for increased anaerobic energy). You get better at producing anaerobic energy, and you get better at buffering the fatigue-producing by-products that accompany it. You'll be able to charge off the start line without fear of running short of energy in the first quarter-mile or staggering to the mile mark when the by-products of un-buffered anaerobic energy production begin shutting down your muscles.

Another benefit is that short reps done at 1500-to-3K pace (see the Training Paces table on p. 128 to get paces; or just guesstimate) recruit 100 percent of your available intermediate muscle fibers and about 80 percent of your fast-twitch fibers. This allows you to strengthen fibers that don't get used during either distance runs or longer repetitions, but which will be recruited in a 5K race. The result is improved leg speed when you need it most in your 5K race.

For maximum 5K racing benefit, you should include 2–3 sessions of short reps per month for a minimum total of 4–5 sessions. Note that short hill reps of 30–60 seconds create a similar stimulus and adaptation, so they can be substituted for traditional interval training. (See more about hill repeats in Key 9.)

Join the
Over-the-Hill Gang

To shine as a 5K runner, you'll need to take to the hills.

If you live in an area with the right terrain, you can add hills to your runs two to three times per month. Your weekly long run is a good choice for hills, since it's bookended by easier training days (adding hills will definitely increase the intensity of distance runs). If you don't have a good hill in your area, consider making occasional hill dates with a treadmill.

Hills have been a staple in the training diets of top distance runners for decades. In the 1960s, famed New Zealand coach Arthur Lydiard used hill training to propel his country's distance runners to international acclaim. In the '70s and '80s, it was Lord Sebastian Coe, two-time Olympic champion at 1500 meters, who relied on hills for the strength that netted him 11 indoor and outdoor world records. And the slopes of the Great Rift Valley have lifted Kenyans to domination of the world distance scene for decades.

These runners included hills in their distance runs for good reason:

- Hills increase the volume of muscle fibers you recruit while running.
- By working more muscle fibers, hill running improves nervous-system coordination between muscle-fiber types, not to mention the muscle groups (e.g., hamstrings and quadriceps) they represent.
- Long hill runs challenge the energy-producing capacity of all fiber types.

▸ Running uphill creates ankle flexibility, improving your stride.

▸ Hill running increases Achilles tendon stiffness, which improves "elastic recoil" (see Key 15 for an explanation of this important running component).

▸ Hill training stimulates adaptations similar to resistance training, and these adaptations improve your ability to produce force.

While distance runs over flat terrain recruit mostly slow-twitch fibers, hill runs draw upon a large percentage of intermediate fibers (and some

Hill Runs vs. Flat Runs			
		LEVEL OF ADAPTATION	
TARGETED BENEFIT		Hill runs	Flat runs
Fiber strength	Slow-twitch	High	High
	Intermediate	Medium	Low
	Fast-twitch	Low	N/A
	Connective tissue	High	Medium
Aerobic energy production	Slow-twitch	High	High
	Intermediate	Medium	Low
	Fast-twitch	Low	N/A
Energy storage (carbs)	Slow-twitch	High	High
	Intermediate	High	Low
	Fast-twitch	Low	N/A
Elastic recoil	Ankle flexibility	Medium	Low
	Elastic recoil	Medium	Low
Nervous system	Muscle-fiber recruitment	Medium	Low
	Muscle-group coordination	Medium	Low

A comparison of hill runs and flat runs shows the increased benefits of the former.

Note: The elevated intensity that accompanies hill runs makes it advisable to treat them like "hard" workouts, with easy days preceding and following them.

fast-twitch fibers) to provide the force required to battle gravity. You put more muscle fibers into action and then work those fibers strenuously. The result? Stronger intermediate and fast-twitch muscle fibers.

Using all these muscle fibers demands increased input from your nervous system. Your nervous system adapts by learning more efficient routes (neural pathways) for communicating commands to muscles and muscle fibers. You develop a more efficient stride that carries over to all your running—uphill, downhill, flat, slow, and fast.

Finally, working all your muscle-fiber types for the prolonged period of time it takes to crest a hill demands a large, sustained energy supply. Your muscles adapt with improvements to both aerobic and anaerobic energy-producing capability. This increased energy supply will help you to sustain a faster pace during your 5K race.

Start by including 5–10 minutes of uphill running in a distance run every 2–3 weeks, then build up to 15–25 minutes of uphill during those runs. And don't race the hills; just run them. (To learn how to structure a super effective hill-rep workout, see Key 9.)

Hills have always been one of the running world's worst-kept training secrets. Almost all elite runners include them. You should, too.

"The fight is won or lost far away from witnesses—behind the lines, in the gym, and out there on the road, long before I dance under those lights."

—Muhammad Ali, three-time heavyweight boxing champion of the world

Schedule Hill Repeats

"Some people train knowing they're not working as hard as other people. I can't fathom how they think."

—Alberto Salazar, three-time New York Marathon champion

Now that we've discussed the benefits of both repetitions and hills, let's combine them to create a super-effective 5K workout: hill repeats. Hill repeats include reps that last between 30 seconds and 2 minutes, with rest intervals (jogging and walking) that are double or triple the length, in time, of the reps.

While workouts like distance and tempo runs, VO_2max reps, and long hill runs trigger adaptations in the number and size of mitochondria in your muscle fibers (i.e., you develop bigger, more numerous mitochondria, thereby increasing aerobic energy–producing potential), intense workouts such as hill repeats turbocharge those mitochondria, significantly increasing their output of aerobic energy. If the workouts already discussed in this book are like outfitting your home with radiant LED security lights, then hill reps are the switch that turns those lights on.

Hill repeats also improve your ability to produce force quickly. That's important because the prime directive each time your foot lands during a stride is to generate enough force to get back into the air. The quicker you do that, the quicker you start your next stride. Generating force is a two-step process. First, you accelerate your foot downward, creating force when your foot collides with the ground. Second, your muscles generate additional force while your foot is on the ground. Because hill repeats shorten the distance your foot travels downward (lessening collision force) and require extra overall force generation to fight gravity, they improve your ability to produce muscular force on the ground. Back on level terrain, the result is a quicker cadence (i.e., more steps per minute) and increased stride length. In other words, you get faster.

Hill repeats also stimulate other training adaptations:

▸ They significantly strengthen all muscle-fiber types.
▸ They rewire your nervous system to recruit all fiber types simultaneously.
▸ They increase your heart's stroke volume.

You'll need to find a hill that's challenging, but not so steep that you can't maintain a good stride. You don't run hill reps by pace. Instead, you target an effort that is slightly more intense than what you'd expect to exert during a 5K race (e.g., 1500–3K effort). Your goal is to finish all reps with a little gas left in the tank—that is, you could probably run one more rep if you had to.

After each rep, turn around and head back down the hill to your start line. Walk for the first 10–15 seconds of your recovery interval, and then jog the rest of the way down. If you reach your start line with time remaining in your recovery interval, do a short walk. For longer recovery intervals, it's okay to stand for 15–30 seconds at the start line after your short walk.

Remember not to turn your hill repeats into a distance run. You need a full recovery, so avoid jogging continuously from the end of one rep until the start of the next. Walk, jog, walk, stand, recover.

Workout Progression for Hill Repeats				
Workout	Number of reps	Length of reps	Recovery interval	Recovery type
1	8–12	30 sec.	1–1.5 min.	Jog/walk
2	10–15	30 sec.	1–1.5 min.	Jog/walk
3	8–12	45 sec.	1.5–2 min.	Jog/walk
4	6–8	60 sec.	2–3 min.	Jog/walk/stand
5	4–6	90 sec.	4–5 min.	Jog/walk/stand

This is a typical progression of hill repeat workouts. Do no more than one session per week. It's OK to skip weeks between sessions.

Hill repeats require intense effort, so one session during a training week is plenty, and no more than two to three sessions per month. The Workout Progression for Hill Repeats table maps out a typical progression of hill-repeat workouts. This progression works even if you skip a week or two between hill rep sessions.

Lengthen
Your Long Run

"The long run is what puts the tiger in the cat."

—*Bill Squires, world-famous distance-running coach*

Once a week, even 5K runners need to go long. It's a common misconception that the length of this long run should be directly proportional to the length of your goal race—that long runs of 90 minutes or more should be left to marathoners. Poppycock. The length of your long run should be based on the physiological demands of your target race. Since 90–95 percent of your 5K-race energy is produced aerobically, you'll want to develop your aerobic system as much as possible. A true long run is a big part of that.

The regular-length distance runs you perform during the week can be counted on to improve aerobic energy production in 70–80 percent of your slow-twitch muscle fibers. But to extend this adaptation to 100 percent of your slow-twitch fibers, as well as a significant percentage of your intermediate fibers, you'll need to schedule one run per week that takes you a little bit farther. Approximately 90 minutes into a distance run, your slow-twitch fibers begin to run out of muscle glycogen (each one of your muscle fibers has its own unique supply of this energy-producing carbohydrate). This forces other slow-twitch fibers—ones not previously recruited—to take over for them. Run long enough, and intermediate fibers are activated, too.

Draining the gas tanks of some fibers while activating other fibers triggers several beneficial adaptations:

▶ Creates new capillaries for all recruited muscle fibers as your body struggles to maintain supply lines over a long period of time

▶ Increases glycogen storage capacity in all affected muscle fibers—your muscle fiber's carbohydrate fuel tanks can double in size

▶ Improves aerobic energy production in all recruited fibers

▶ Improves ability to burn fat as an energy source (you won't burn much fat during a 5K, but burning fat more efficiently spares glycogen during both normal training and your race-day warm-up)

▶ Increases supply of aerobic enzymes (these enzymes facilitate aerobic energy production)

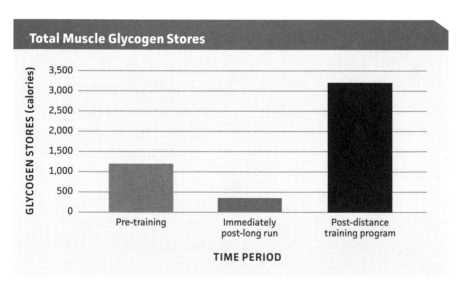

By depleting your glycogen stores significantly during your long run, you help trigger an adaptation that leads to greater glycogen storage in the future.

▸ Improves nervous-system control of recruited fibers, leading to a more efficient stride
▸ Strengthens recruited muscle fibers and connective tissue

Of course, the 5K isn't the marathon, so you won't need runs that stretch to 20 miles or more. That would be a misuse of your running body's precious capacity to recover and rebuild. But runs that last 90–120 minutes will go a long way to ensuring you develop the aerobic energy-producing capacity required for a faster 5K.

Two rules of thumb to help you plan your long runs:

1 Your long run should account for 15–25 percent of your week's total volume.
2 Your long run should not exceed 150 percent of the length of your regular distance runs, although this rule can be broken for low-mileage runners or those who train less than 5 days per week.

Bottom line: Run long and prosper.

Try Downhill Running

Nothing strengthens your quadriceps for running more effectively than downhill strides or downhill tempo.

Nothing.

These workouts require you to run downhill at an accelerated pace, thereby increasing the intensity of eccentric muscle contractions associated with running.

An eccentric muscle contraction occurs when a muscle both contracts and stretches at the same time. An eccentric contraction of your quadriceps occurs every time your foot touches down during a running stride. Your front thigh contracts to brake and support you, but it simultaneously stretches to allow your knee to bend. In contrast, a concentric contraction occurs when a muscle contracts and shortens (e.g., when you show off your guns by flexing your biceps, bunching the shortened muscle into a ball).

It's important to include eccentric training in your program for two reasons:

1 Eccentric contractions produce substantially more force than concentric contractions, increasing the training load for the muscle fibers that are activated.
2 Eccentric contractions are associated with post-workout muscle soreness (called DOMS, or delayed onset muscle soreness), so you'll want to immunize your legs against that possibility.

While there are several theories for why eccentric contractions produce more force than concentric ones, the important takeaway for runners is that this increased force is produced while recruiting fewer muscle fibers. That's right: You generate more force using less muscle. By running downhill, you increase the eccentric load even more. You give your legs a workout that can't be matched on flat ground. Your leg muscles, especially your quadriceps, respond by getting stronger. A lot stronger. While other runners' legs might be sore the day after a hard speed workout or a race, yours will feel fresh and bouncy.

Downhill running also strengthens both connective tissue and your nervous system's control of muscle contractions, improving what's known as "leg stiffness." Leg stiffness doesn't refer to post-workout muscle stiffness or a lack of flexibility. Instead, it's a measure of your leg's resistance to bending at the ankles, knees, and hips when your foot touches the ground. Less bending means less energy loss, less time

Workout Progression for Downhill Running

Workout	Number of reps	Length of reps	Effort level	Recovery
1	4–6	15–30 sec.	Tempo	Walk back to start
2	6–8	15–30 sec.	10K	Walk back to start
3	8–10	15–30 sec.	5K	Walk back to start
4	1	5 min.	Tempo	5+ min. jog
5	1	8–10 min.	Tempo	5+ min. jog
6	1	10–12 min.	Tempo	5+ min. jog

Begin your downhill training with tempo-effort reps, then increase both number of reps and intensity over the next sessions. If desired, advance to a single downhill tempo rep, with a jog recovery.

Note: No more than one session per week.

spent on the ground, and a more efficient stride. Think of bouncing a super ball (leg stiffness) versus a beach ball (untrained legs).

Additionally, you'll improve your knee lift, stride length, and cadence (the number of steps you take per minute).

As a bonus, eccentric training requires less energy and less nervous system input than a similarly intense workout on flat ground. After initial muscle strengthening, you'll require less recovery after a session of downhill running than following a hard track workout.

So we're clear, you won't get these benefits from the normal downhill running you'll log during distance runs. Instead, you'll have to schedule sessions of more intense downhill training (no more than one session per week):

Downhill strides: Start with a set of 4–6 strides, 15–30 seconds each, at about 80–85 percent maximum effort (tempo effort) on a semi-steep hill. Walk back to the start line for recovery. Add two strides per workout, up to a maximum of 10.

Downhill tempo: After you've completed at least three weeks of downhill strides, try a continuous downhill tempo run. Start with 5 minutes of tempo, then build over successive workouts to 10–12 minutes. If you don't have a long hill in your area, you can substitute longer downhill reps, still at tempo effort (don't run harder than tempo effort for reps over 30 seconds).

One of the best things about downhill running is that the training sticks with you. Once you've gotten the adaptation you're after, you'll only have to schedule downhill running once a month to retain its benefits.

A note of warning: Masters runners should exercise caution when performing this workout, as hamstring strains can occur in older runners during intense downhill running. For these runners, a more conservative pace and less aggressive week-to-week progression is advised. Runners with a history of hamstring issues should skip this workout altogether.

"Toenails are overrated." —*Unknown runner*

Perform Goal-Pace Repetitions at the Right Time

Lots of 5K runners perform track repetitions (e.g., 400-meter reps) at their goal 5K pace.

Most of these same 5K runners do their goal-pace reps too early in their training schedule. Instead of getting a race benefit, they risk sabotaging their 5K programs.

Training at goal pace before you've achieved goal-pace fitness overtaxes your nervous system, muscles, connective tissue, and energy systems. While you may experience a short-lived bump in fitness, the excessive load this training places on your body can lead to fatigue, injury, illness, or overtraining syndrome (see Key 19). At best, you simply fail to improve.

While you're in the fitness-building phase of running, your 5K-effort repetitions should be based on current fitness. Current fitness means the pace you could run for 5K that day. During this phase of training, you're not running repetitions to practice pace; you're using pace as a way to target the specific percentage of VO_2max represented by that pace. That allows you to control which muscle-fiber types and energy systems you train.

This guideline changes, however, as race day approaches and you begin to acquire goal fitness. Now, it's time to fine-tune your 5K engine. Your nervous system needs to become efficient at orchestrating your goal-pace stride, and you want to develop conscious recognition of various sensations at goal pace. By becoming familiar with the visual and audible cues associated with goal pace (such as the visual of whizzing past trees, houses, and parked cars on the road, or the audible cue of your shoes' cadence on the ground), you'll find it easier to recognize and implement that pace during an actual race. This will help you resist both an adrenaline-fueled sprint off the start (see Key 24) and the impulse to match the pace of competitors who are running faster than you want to go.

You'll want your first goal-pace workout to include shorter reps and plenty of rest. These shorter reps help your nervous system lock onto the pace. For your next goal-pace workouts, you'll lengthen the reps, cutting down the recovery interval for reps of 400 meters or less (these latter workouts are referenced in Key 6 on VO_2max, and they provide a huge VO_2max stimulus). These workouts both prepare your nervous system for goal pace and build aerobic strength.

The Goal-Pace Repetitions Progression table provides a template for a workout-to-workout progression. Or you can create your own repetition workouts. Just be sure to limit individual reps to a maximum of 1600 meters-per-rep (or 1 mile on the roads or trail), allow a recovery interval of 50–100 percent of the length (in time) of your reps, and target a total volume (for all reps combined) of between 4,800 and 8,000 meters.

"You learn to cut down trees by cutting them down." —*Bateke proverb*

Goal-Pace Repetitions Progression					
Workout	Sets	Reps per set	Length of reps	Effort level	Recovery
1	2	6	200m	5K for 1st set; 3K for 2nd set	200m slow jog between reps; 400m jog between sets
2	1	10–12	400m	5K	200m slow jog
3	1	12–16	400m	5K	100m slow jog
4	1	6–8	800m	5K	400m slow jog
5	1	16–20	400m	5K	100m slow jog
6	1	6–8	1000m	5K	3 min. jog
7	1	16–20	400m	5K	100m slow jog
8	1	3–5	1600m	5K	3 min. jog

This is a sample progression of goal-pace repetition workouts. You don't have to perform this entire progression. It's OK to pick and choose workouts from this schedule (or create your own), although you should include the first two workouts, as they are essential for teaching your nervous system goal pace.

Run a 5K Tune-Up Race

No single workout will prepare you better for your goal race than a 5K tune-up race.

That's because you won't be able to run a faster 5K until you run a slower one.

Your brain won't let you.

It's your brain's job to regulate the amount of exercise and effort your body experiences. And, much like an overprotective parent, your brain is afraid you're going to hurt yourself. It believes that, if left to your own devices, you'll run so hard that your body temperature will soar, your heart explode, and your muscles and connective tissue be damaged beyond repair.

According to the Central Governor Theory, proposed by South African exercise scientist Dr. Timothy Noakes, "the brain regulates exercise performance by continuously modifying the number of motor units [i.e., a nerve and the muscle fibers it controls] that are recruited in the exercising limbs." In layman's terms, this means that your brain shuts down muscle fibers if it thinks you're working too hard or running too low on fuel. Furthermore, Noakes claims that the brain anticipates danger before it arrives, acting preemptively to avoid it. It does this by creating a sensation of fatigue and decreasing the force your muscles can generate.

The good news is that your brain can be taught that a 5K race isn't dangerous. You accomplish this by running an entire 5K race without killing yourself. The brain responds by letting you run harder—and faster—the next time out.

Tune-up races help your 5K goal race preparation in other ways, too:

- ▸ You gain experience dealing with pre-race jitters.
- ▸ You gain experience dealing with common pre-race activities such as finding a parking spot, lining up for the Porta Potty, and securing your timing chip to your shoe.
- ▸ You practice adhering to a sensible race plan.
- ▸ You learn to shrug off bad weather and other unforeseen obstacles.

You can run a tune-up 5K two weeks before your goal 5K and expect to be recovered for your target race (it's possible to race again in a week, as long as you exclude hard workouts in the interim, but most runners benefit from a short period of training between tune-up and goal races). If you can't find a tune-up 5K, it's okay to pick a different race distance. Just make sure that if you race longer than 5K (e.g., a 10K or half-marathon), you also allot more recovery time before your goal race. How much time? See the Post-Tune-Up Race Recovery Time chart.

"One must learn by doing the thing, for though you think you know it, you have no certainty, until you try." —Sophocles

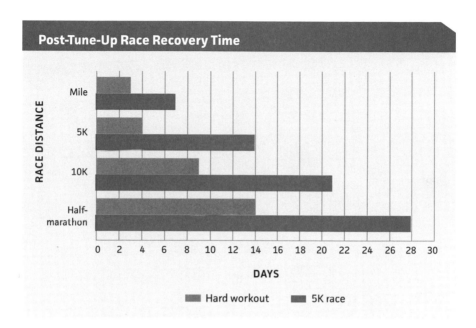

Post-Tune-Up Race Recovery Time

This chart suggests post-race recovery periods for races of various distances. The gray line represents the number of days before runners should perform their first hard workout. The orange line suggests the days runners should wait before a goal 5K race.

Schedule Injury-Prevention Exercises & Resistance Training

You can't run a fast 5K if you're injured.

And chances are good that you'll join the 50–80 percent of runners who get injured every year if you neglect to set aside the time for two important components of your training:

1 A 10–15-minute post-run injury-prevention routine that includes rope stretching and easy body exercises, done 2–3 times per week
2 A 30–60-minute injury-prevention and resistance training routine, done 1–2 times per week during base training

Unfortunately, injury-prevention exercises don't double as injury-reversal routines.

When it comes to injuries, there's good news and bad news.

The bad news is that millions of runners each year fail to meet their running goals—say, a fast 5K—because they get injured. They get sidelined with runner's knee, Achilles pain, plantar fasciitis, IT band syndrome, lower back pain, or some other disabling injury. (See the Estimated Number of Running Injuries Per Year for 5K Race Finishers chart for a breakdown of the breakdowns.)

The good news is that you can reduce the likelihood of injury by including prevention and resistance routines in your program. The better news is that these routines also make you faster. A 2015 study published in the *International Journal of Sports Physiology and Performance* concluded that only six weeks of resistance training "significantly improves 5-km time." And a 2013 study on masters marathoners found that six weeks of resistance training improved running economy by 6 percent—running economy measures the amount of oxygen you use to maintain a specific pace; improved economy means you can use less oxygen (energy) to run that pace, giving you the option of either running faster or maintaining the pace for longer (at the same oxygen cost). Other adaptations you can expect include:

▸ Improved muscle balance
▸ Increased stride length
▸ Increased cadence (steps per minute)
▸ Improved stability
▸ Improved core strength

One final bit of advice about injury-prevention exercises: They aren't competitions. Don't try to do them better than anyone has ever done them before. They're "checkmark" work—something you complete and then check off your to-do list. If you work them too hard, you just might end up suffering the injuries you're trying to avoid.

"A clever person solves a problem. A wise person avoids it." —Anonymous

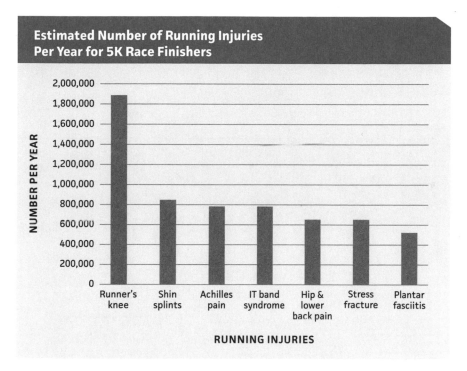

Estimated Number of Running Injuries Per Year for 5K Race Finishers

This is the estimated number of training and race injuries suffered by the 10 million 5K race finishers in the United States each year, based on an injury rate of 65 percent (estimates range from 50–80 percent).

POST-RUN STRETCHING & EXERCISE ROUTINE

FREQUENCY: 2–3 times per week

WHEN: Post-workout (best after distance runs)

DURATION: Approximately 10–15 minutes

TOWEL TOE CURLS

Towel toe curls strengthen muscles in your feet and help keep plantar fasciitis at bay. Plantar fasciitis is usually felt as pain in your heel or your arch.

1 Sit barefoot in a chair, knees at a 90-degree angle, with toes resting on the near edge of a towel spread flat on the floor. Put a shoe on the far edge of the towel to provide resistance.

2 Keeping your heels on the floor, scrunch your toes to drag the towel toward you. Bunch the towel beneath your arch (then behind your heels when it builds up under your arch) until you've pulled in the towel's entire length.

▸▸ *Repeat twice.*

LEG LIFTS

Leg lifts strengthen your abs and hip flexors, leading to core stability and better knee lift.

1 Lie on your back with knees slightly bent. Link your hands behind your head, lifting your head off the floor/ground.

2 Keeping your torso stable and maintaining the angle of your knees, lift your legs to 45 degrees, then lower at a controlled (not slow) rate. Just before your heels touch the ground, lift them again for the next rep.

▸▸ *Start with one set of 15–20 reps, then build up over the course of several weeks to one set of 40–50 reps.*

ROPE HAMSTRING STRETCH

Stretching post-run can reduce stiffness for the next day's run. But don't overstretch—your muscles aren't taffy. You're simply teaching your nervous system that it's safe to allow your hamstrings a little more range of motion.

1 Lie on your back with one knee bent, foot flat on the floor. Hook a rope (or belt, rolled towel, etc.) around the arch of your opposite foot, with that leg extended (a small bend at the knee is OK).

2 Holding the ends of the rope in your hands, gently pull to raise the leg until you reach your full range of motion (don't overstretch!). Simultaneously flex your quadriceps muscle, as this helps relax the hamstring. Hold for 30 seconds, then lower the leg and repeat with the opposite leg.

▸▸ *Do one rep for each leg.*

ROPE CALF STRETCH

Like the rope hamstring stretch, this exercise will reduce calf stiffness for your next run. It will also help stave off calf tightness, soreness, and strains that sometimes follow intense workouts.

1 Lie on your back with one knee bent, foot flat on the floor. Hook a rope (or belt, rolled towel, etc.) around the ball (front portion, excluding toes) of your opposite foot, with that leg extended (a small bend at the knee is OK).

2 While flexing your quadriceps, hold the ends of the rope in your hands and gently pull to lift the leg and angle your foot toward your shin (don't pull too hard!). Hold for 30 seconds, then lower the leg and repeat with the opposite leg.

▸▸ *Do one rep for each leg.*

BONUS: THE DAYDREAMER

If lower back pain and tightness is a problem, add the daydreamer to your routine. For this exercise, the key word is "relax." Don't do anything except maintain the position.

1 Lie on your back with your arms out to your sides, hands at approximately belly level, feet propped on a chair, with a 90-degree bend at your knees and waist. Try to keep your feet from rolling outward (they can rest against the chair back).

▸▸ *Take slow, deep breaths, relax, and hold for 5–10 minutes.*

INJURY-PREVENTION & RESISTANCE TRAINING ROUTINE

FREQUENCY: 1–2 times per week

WHEN: Post-workout (best after distance runs)

DURATION: Approximately 30–60 minutes

AIR SQUATS OR SQUATS (WITH WEIGHTS)

Runners without previous (and recent) resistance-training experience should start with air squats, and then switch to squats (with weight) when their fitness improves. Squats work your glutes, quadriceps, and hamstrings. Runners will see better results from quarter-squats than half- or full-squats. Our knees don't bend much while running, so they don't need to bend much during squats.

AIR SQUATS

1 Stand with feet hip-width apart, toes pointed slightly out, with arms straight out from your shoulders.

2 Bend your knees, pushing your hips back until the bend at the back of your knees is between 135 degrees (quarter-squat) and 90 degrees (half-squat). Simultaneously bring your arms forward, which helps you maintain balance. Push upward to return to your start position.

▶▶ *Do 2–3 sets of 5–12 reps, depending on your fitness.*

SQUATS

1 Stand straight with a barbell resting on your shoulders, hands wider than shoulder-width on the bar (you can hold dumbbells in each hand, if you prefer). Feet should be hip-width apart, toes pointing slightly out.

2 Keep your feet flat, and move your hips back while bending your knees. Lower your torso to a quarter-squat (or half-squat). Don't arch your back or perform the exercise too quickly. When you reach the squat position, reverse the motion to return to your starting position.

▶▶ *Do 2–4 sets of 8–10 reps, depending on your fitness.*

STEP-DOWNS

Step-downs work your quadriceps eccentrically, strengthening them for the load they'll encounter when your foot touches down during each stride. Combined with squats, step-downs help stabilize your knee, important for preventing runner's knee.

1 Balance on one foot at the edge of a platform (bench, step, etc.), with the ball of your foot extended over the platform's edge. Hold onto a nearby object for balance—this is about working the quadriceps, not working balance. Suspend the opposite leg, knee straight, with your foot in front of the platform.

2 Lower your hips by bending your support leg until the bend at the back of your knee is at approximately 135 degrees (90 degrees is too much). Your free foot will lower in front of the platform (as if you're stepping down). Rise back to your starting position and repeat.

⏵ *Do 5–10 reps, depending upon your fitness, then repeat with your other leg. Do 1–2 sets.*

STEP-UPS

Step-ups target concentric contractions of your glutes, quadriceps, and hamstrings. This exercise helps you generate the force required to take off from the ground during each stride. It also puts your muscles through a fuller range of motion than squats or step-downs.

1 Stand in front of a platform (bench, box, step, etc.). Place your right foot on the platform with your left foot flat on the ground. Start with the knee and hip of your raised leg at 90 degrees (bending more than 90 degrees is dangerous for your knees).
2 With your arms at your sides, push with your right leg to extend (straighten) your hip and knee as you rise up on the platform. Momentarily rest the ball of your left foot on the platform, and then reverse your motion to return to your starting position.

⏵ *Do 5–10 reps, depending upon your fitness, then repeat with your other leg. Do 1–2 sets.*

SINGLE-LEG DEADLIFTS

Single-leg deadlifts are one of two exercises that work the hamstrings eccentrically. The hamstrings endure eccentric loads of up to 10 times body weight during each stride, so it's essential that you strengthen them. You can do this exercise with or without weight. If you use weight, hold a dumbbell in the opposite hand from your down leg.

1 With your feet hip-width apart, lift your right foot off the ground by bending your knee. Bend your left knee slightly—don't do this exercise straight-legged. Use a chair or other object for balance.

2 Bend forward from your hips, reaching your right hand toward the ground in front of your left foot. Simultaneously lift and extend your right leg behind you. Maintain a slight bend in both knees. Now, in one smooth motion, return to your starting position, contracting your glutes and hamstrings. Use your hips as a hinge as you swing during this exercise (think of the Drinking Bird toy).

▸▸ *Do 5–10 reps, depending upon your fitness, then repeat with your other leg. Do 1–2 sets.*

NORDIC CURLS

This is your second eccentric hamstring exercise. While single-leg dead-lifts focus on the upper hamstrings and glutes, Nordic curls target the lower hamstrings.

1 Kneel, with elbows at your sides and hands held at chest height (as if you're about to do a push-up). You'll need a partner or a sturdy object to hold your ankles in place.

2 Bend forward from your knees, keeping hips and back straight, slowly lowering yourself toward the ground. If you start to fall (i.e., if your hamstrings can't support your weight at some point in the exercise), use your hands to slow your descent.

3 Use your arms to thrust yourself back up to your starting position. Don't attempt to return to your starting position

by contracting your hamstrings—that's an injury begging to happen.

▸▸ *Do 1–2 sets of 2–10 reps (start with low reps, slowly build up to more reps).*

HEEL DIPS

Heel dips will give you stiffer and stronger Achilles tendons. This eccentric exercise protects you against Achilles tendinitis, Achilles tendinosis, Achilles bursitis, and Achilles insertional problems. Unlike other injury-prevention exercises, heel dips can also double as a cure.

1 Balance on the balls of your feet on a platform (bench, box, step, etc.). Your heels should extend over the edge of the platform. Use a rail or other support for balance. As your fitness improves, hold a dumbbell in the same side hand as your working leg.

2 Raise up on your toes, shift all your weight to your right foot, then slowly lower your right heel through its full range of motion. Your left foot can rest lightly on the platform, or you can raise it off the platform as long as you maintain balance. Don't do this exercise too slowly, just slowly enough to control the motion.

3 Use both feet to quickly rise back to your start position. This isn't about working your calves (i.e., it's not a calf-raise exercise). It's about eccentrically lowering your heel. If you don't have a platform—or pain prevents you from lowering your heel through its full range of motion—it's okay to do this exercise on level ground (or the floor). Do all reps with one foot before switching to the other.

▸▸ *Start with 1–2 sets of 5 reps each foot, then build to 2–3 sets of 20 reps.*

PLANKS

The plank is the best exercise for strengthening all the muscles of your core—front, sides, and back—and it improves spinal stabilization.

1   Start in a modified push-up position: face down, resting on elbows and toes, with your elbows directly beneath your shoulders, a 90-degree bend at your elbows with your forearms extended forward. Maintain a straight line from your head through your toes.

▸▸ *Hold the position, squeezing your glutes and tightening your abdominals for 30–60 seconds. One repetition is enough.*

Schedule Technique Drills & Plyometrics

Technique drills and plyometrics are two types of training that most runners ignore. That's a mistake. Both make you faster and improve your running economy. By combining them, you can get a leg up on (and a stride ahead of) the competition.

Technique drills, also called form drills, isolate and exaggerate elements of your stride. The goal is to strengthen the muscles involved in your stride, increase your range of motion, fine-tune neuromuscular function, and improve elastic recoil, which we'll define in a minute.

Plyometrics, sometimes referred to as "jump training," usually involves dropping to the ground from an elevated height, absorbing the landing force, and then springing back into the air. It triggers adaptations in explosive strength, nervous-system reaction time, and running economy.

Combined into a single session—as either a standalone workout or the prelude to a short repetitions or hill repeats workout—drills and plyometrics will improve your stride rate, stride length, and stride efficiency, while training two components of running that often go overlooked:

Elastic recoil: When your foot touches down with each stride, your tendons, muscles, and ligaments stretch, absorbing the energy produced by gravity and motion. Running mechanics expert and author Jay Dicharry has described this as pulling back a slingshot. Once your foot passes under your body, you release this energy, which helps catapult you into your next stride. This is equivalent to releasing the slingshot. Since your muscles don't generate this energy (once you're up to speed), it's "free." And it accounts for about 50 percent of the energy you'll use to fuel each stride, with your Achilles tendon alone providing up to 35 percent. When you improve elastic recoil with drills, you get a longer, stronger, more energy-efficient stride.

Stretch-shortening cycle: In a stretch-shortening cycle, an eccentric contraction of a muscle (the muscle contracts while it lengthens) is followed immediately by a concentric contraction (the muscle contracts as it shortens). The result is a significant increase in the force created by the latter contraction. Stretch-shortening cycles occur multiple times during each stride (e.g., your hamstrings experience a stretch-shortening cycle just before your foot touches the ground, and your calves do the same from the moment your foot lands until you start to take off again). Plyometrics trains your body to better utilize these cycles. You'll generate greater force at an accelerated rate, which translates to less time spent on the ground.

Research has shown that plyometrics is even more effective than resistance training for improving running economy in endurance runners. If you really want that fast 5K, however, you'll do both.

The following training session utilizes drills that include a plyometric component.

TECHNIQUE DRILLS (including plyometric component)

FREQUENCY: 1 time per week

WHEN: Before short repetitions or hill repeats, or as a standalone workout bookended by distance run days

DURATION: 30–40 minutes (1 rep of each drill)

Note: Perform these in the order listed.

SKIPPING

Step forward with one foot, spring off it, land on it again, spring off it again, then land on the other foot and repeat. Just like when you were a kid in the schoolyard.

▸ *Do one rep of 20–60 meters (depending on fitness), then jog back to the start line, immediately perform a stride (at 85–90 percent maximum speed) for the same distance, then walk back to the start line.*

HIGH SKIPPING

When you skip this time, go for height and don't worry about how far forward each skip takes you. Spring high off your toes, then land on the same foot before stepping forward into your next high skip.

▸ *Do one rep of 20–60 meters. Jog back. Stride. Walk back.*

LONG SKIPPING (plyometric drill)

Skip again, this time going for distance, not height. Take off on one foot, land on the same foot, then just step into the next skip (i.e., you spring far during the skip, not so far when you're switching feet).

▶▶ *Do one rep of 20–60 meters. Jog back. Stride. Walk back.*

FLAT-FOOTED MARCHING

March forward, lifting knees toward your chest, while keeping your down foot flat on the ground (i.e., don't come up on the ball of your foot as you march forward). Swing arms in sync with the marching (i.e., right leg and left arm forward, then left leg and right arm forward). Land each marching step flat-footed. Keep a piston-like motion as you drive your knees up and down.

▶▶ *Do one rep of 20–60 meters. Jog back. Stride. Walk back.*

HIGH KNEES

Stay on the balls of your feet as you move forward, driving one knee and then the other toward your chest, simultaneously driving the ball of your opposite foot into the ground—this latter action creates a spring-like effect (elastic recoil) as your Achilles tendon absorbs and releases energy. Move your legs as quickly as you can.

▶▶ *Do one rep of 20–60 meters. Jog back. Stride. Walk back.*

BOUNDING (plyometric drill)

This is a great exercise for both elastic recoil and developing strong stretch-shortening cycles. Drive forward off the ball of one foot, trying for a combination of distance and height, hover in the air, then land on your opposite foot, quickly absorb the landing force, and drive forward off that foot.

▸▸ *Alternate legs with each bound, for 20–60 meters. Jog back. Stride. Walk back.*

QUICK FEET

Quickly lift one foot and move it forward 1–3 inches. Repeat with the other foot.

▸▸ *Move your feet as quickly as you can, inching forward until you've covered 20–30 meters. Walk forward an additional 20 meters. Jog back. Stride. Walk back.*

QUICK HOPS (plyometric drill)

Like bounding, this is a great drill for both elastic recoil and stretch-shortening cycles. Keep feet together as you spring forward with short hops. The emphasis is on springing forward, not up.

▸▸ *Cover 20–30 meters. Walk forward an additional 20 meters. Jog back. Stride. Walk back.*

BUTT KICKS

Run tall, staying on the balls of your feet. You'll keep your thighs mostly perpendicular to the ground while kicking your heels back, attempting to touch your butt (it's okay if you come up short). Work arms in a running motion. Don't strain during this drill.

▸▸ *Do one rep of 20–60 meters. Jog back. Stride. Walk back.*

"The foot feels the foot when it feels the ground."

—Ernest Wood, English yogi, theosophist, and author

Effect of Resistance Training & Plyometrics on Running Economy & Performance

Beginning 5K time (A)	Post–RT: 5K time (B)	Post–RT + Plyo: 5K time (C)
15:00	14:33–14:46	14:10–14:35
16:00	15:31–15:46	15:07–15:34
17:00	16:29–16:45	16:04–16:32
18:00	17:28–17:44	17:01–17:30
19:00	18:26–18:43	17:57–18:29
20:00	19:24–19:42	18:54–19:27
21:00	20:22–20:41	19:51–20:25
22:00	21:20–21:40	20:47–21:24
23:00	22:19–22:39	21:44–22:22
24:00	23:17–23:38	22:41–23:20
25:00	24:15–24:37	23:37–24:19
26:00	25:13–25:37	24:34–25:17
27:00	26:11–26:36	25:31–26:15
28:00	27:10–27:35	26:28–27:14
29:00	28:08–28:34	27:24–28:12
30:00	29:06–29:33	28:21–29:11
31:00	30:04–30:32	29:18–30:09
32:00	31:02–31:31	30:14–31:07
33:00	32:01–32:30	31:11–32:06
34:00	32:59–33:29	32:08–33:04
35:00	33:57–34:28	33:05–34:02
36:00	34:55–35:28	34:01–35:01
37:00	35:53–36:27	34:58–35:59
38:00	36:52–37:26	35:55–36:57
39:00	37:50–38:25	36:51–37:56
40:00	38:48–39:24	37:48–38:54
45:00	43:39–44:20	42:31–43:46

Resistance training (RT) and plyometrics improve performance by improving running economy. Find a time close to your current 5K time in Column A. Columns B and C offer a range of the times you can expect to run after 8–12 weeks of either resistance training or resistance training plus plyometrics.

Note: Improved times are given in a range, as some athletes respond better than others. Also, note that athletes who already have a well-rounded program won't see as much improvement.

LIFESTYLE,
DIET & GEAR
KEYS

Eat a Runner's Diet

The first rule for planning your runner's diet is simple: Make sure you get enough of everything you need. That means enough carbohydrates, enough fat, and enough protein.

The 5K race is a high-intensity endurance event, and both your training and racing will need to be powered by plentiful, quality fuel.

Your diet starts with carbohydrates. Carbohydrates are the fuel that drives 5K performance. In fact, carbs (stored in your muscles and liver as glycogen) provide between 75–90 percent of the fuel you'll use to produce energy during your 5K race.

Your starting glycogen level also helps determine the fatigue you'll feel during training and racing. When your initial glycogen levels are low, your brain responds by limiting your ability to exercise intensely. When they're high, there are no such restrictions. A hard workout will reduce your muscle glycogen levels by 50–85 percent (see Total Muscle Glycogen Stores, Key 10). It will reduce your liver glycogen stores, which fuel your nervous system, even more. So it's imperative that you include lots of carbs in your daily diet. Studies indicate that it takes a minimum of 22 hours to restock glycogen, but you can jump-start the process by consuming about 50 grams (200 calories) of carbs right after your workout, when your body stores glycogen at an accelerated rate. After that, you'll want to keep your carb intake high, aiming for between 2.3 and 5.5 grams (i.e., 9.2 and 22 calories) of carbohydrates per pound of body weight per day, depending on the volume and intensity of your training. If you train more than once per day, you'll want at least one of those

"Exercise is king. Nutrition is queen. Put them together and you've got a kingdom." —Jack LaLanne, American fitness, exercise, and nutrition expert

workouts to be low intensity (e.g., an easy-paced, short distance run), as low-intensity exercise splits its fuel source more evenly between carbs and fats. One thing is certain: If you skimp on carbohydrates, you'll limit your ability to train, and you'll run slower during your 5K race.

Fat is your second source of energy, accounting for about 50 percent of the calories you'll burn during distance runs (and an even larger percentage during your weekly long run, during which glycogen becomes scarce and your body turns to this denser source of energy). While most of us already possess an almost inexhaustible fat supply (love handles, anyone?), that doesn't mean you should minimize fat in your diet. Your body becomes efficient at burning the types of fuel you consume. If you eat fat, you'll be better able to use fat during exercise. That translates to better training and better performance. In fact, research has found a significant performance improvement for runners whose diets included at least 30 percent fat. A 2008 study concluded that women who failed to meet the 30 percent threshold were 250 percent more likely to get injured.

Last but not least, proteins are the building blocks for your cells and hormones, and they're essential to post-workout repair. "If you take a big spike of protein before bed," says exercise scientist and elite-level coach Steve Magness, "you'll get a huge spike in protein synthesis overnight—when a bunch of muscle repair and recovery goes on." Magness recommends 30 grams of protein before bed, with up to five additional 15-gram servings of protein throughout the day. As a 5K athlete, you'll want a protein intake of about 0.6 to 0.9 grams per pound of body weight per day.

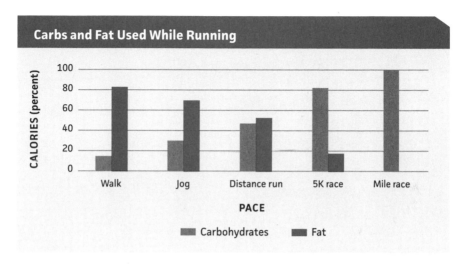

Different training intensities burn different combinations of carbs and fat. While walking is mostly fueled by fat, a timed mile is fueled entirely by carbs. The 5K gets most of its energy from carbs, but fat provides 10–25 percent (depending on your pace) of the calories you'll burn.

Of course, you can't live on macronutrients alone. You'll also need to meet the RDA requirements for vitamins and minerals (the RDA is appropriate for 97–98 percent of healthy people). But don't reach for the supplement shelf. Instead, get your nutrition—your carbs, fats, proteins, vitamins, and minerals—from real food, served in its original state (e.g., apples, not packaged fruit pies). When you eat enough of the right foods, you give your body the raw materials it requires to build your best 5K body.

Run Light

The simplest way to ensure a faster 5K is to run light. Weight loss of even five pounds can improve your 5K time by anywhere from 15 seconds to a minute.

Of course, before you go on a diet, you need to determine how much weight you need to lose—or if you need to lose weight at all. While healthy weight loss will lead to better running performance, it does no good to diet if you're currently at a fit, thin, competition weight.

A quick way to gauge whether you're a candidate for weight loss is to calculate your BMI. Before doing that, understand that BMI is a limited tool. According to the Centers for Disease Control (CDC), "BMI does not distinguish between excess fat, muscle, or bone mass," and it fails to account for such factors as age, sex, and ethnicity. Muscular people and athletes often have a high BMI without being unhealthy, and women tend to have more total body fat than men with the same BMI. Still, it's a simple way to ballpark your weight-loss potential, with studies showing a strong correlation to more direct measures of fat. To calculate BMI:

- ▶ Multiply your weight (in pounds) by 703.
- ▶ Divide the answer by your height in inches.
- ▶ Divide again by your height in inches—this is your BMI.
- ▶ If your multiplication and division skills are sketchy, there are plenty of online calculators ready to do the work for you (just do an online search for "BMI calculator").

"Sweat is fat crying." —Anonymous

If your BMI is between 18.5 and 24.9, then congratulations—you're healthy. Below that is underweight. If you're over that range, take a closer look at your training diet.

If you believe you're a candidate for healthy weight loss, you can look forward to multiple benefits. Healthy weight loss increases VO_2max, reduces the impact forces absorbed by your muscles and connective tissue, and improves running economy. You get fitter and faster.

That said, be aware that there are short-term drawbacks.

First, dieting lowers stored muscle glycogen levels. Lower muscle glycogen levels reduce the effort you can maintain during both training and racing. A 2001 study comparing two groups of cyclists—one who began a time trial with elevated glycogen levels and one who began with non-elevated levels—found that, although both groups started at the same pace, the non-elevated group reduced speed within a minute, eventually finishing 6 percent slower than the glycogen-primed group (even as both groups had almost identical levels of remaining glycogen at the time trial's conclusion).

Next, losing weight too quickly—or when you're already thin—can result in the loss of lean muscle mass. Skeletal muscle powers your movement, so reduced muscle-fiber size lessens the force available for that movement. You risk negating any benefits derived from weight loss since you simultaneously lose energy and power.

Finally, dieting can lower your metabolism by as much as 20 percent. Your metabolism includes all the processes through which your body uses food to create energy and maintain bodily functions. It accounts for the majority of calories you use each day. You need to burn 3,500 calories

The Influence of Healthy Weight Loss on 5K Time								
YOUR WEIGHT	**CURRENT 5K TIME: 15:00**		**CURRENT 5K TIME: 20:00**		**CURRENT 5K TIME: 25:00**		**CURRENT 5K TIME: 30:00**	
	- 5 lb.	**- 10 lb.**	**- 5 lb.**	**- 10 lb.**	**- 5 lb.**	**- 10 lb.**	**- 5 lb.**	**- 10 lb.**
120	14:33	14:01	19:24	18:42	24:14	23:22	29:05	28:03
160	14:41	14:17	19:34	19:03	24:28	23:48	29:21	28:34
200	14:45	14:26	19:41	19:15	24:36	24:04	29:31	28:53
240	14:49	14:32	19:45	19:23	24:41	24:14	29:37	29:05

This table illustrates how much time runners at various 5K times might improve with healthy weight loss of 5 or 10 pounds, based on sample body weights.

more than you consume to lose one pound, so a lowered metabolism can turn a difficult diet goal into an impossible one.

Now for the good news.

As discussed in Key 16, your body replaces muscle glycogen at an accelerated rate following training, so a carb infusion within 30 minutes post-run helps stock your muscles with glycogen for the next workout, even if you skimp on calories for the rest of the day.

Next, you can minimize the loss of lean muscle mass by following two easy guidelines. One, target weight loss of no more than 1–2 pounds per week. Two, perform high-intensity workouts (e.g., resistance training) that reinforce previous strength gains.

Finally, there is a silver bullet solution for keeping your metabolism high while you diet: exercise. Daily exercise will counteract most of the effect that dieting has on metabolism.

Don't panic if you don't see weight loss right away. Eventually, faced with a combination of calorie restriction and exercise, your metabolism will blink, and you'll be on your way to your weight-loss goal—and a faster 5K.

Wear Light Racing Flats

"The man who moves a mountain begins by carrying away small stones."

—*Adapted from a fable by Liè Zi, Taoist philosopher*

Here's a quick way to drop a minimum of 9–18 seconds from your 5K time without having to train or diet: Race in a lighter pair of shoes.

Research has found that decreasing the weight of your racing shoes by 3.5 ounces per shoe will improve your 5K time by about 1 percent. The average training shoe weighs 11–12 ounces, while most racing flats tip the scales at about 6–8 ounces, with the lightest racing flats boasting a barely there 4 ounces. By switching from training shoes to the lightest flats, a 20-minute 5K runner can cut about 24 seconds from his or her time—12 seconds if he or she is already racing in 7–8-ounce flats. A 30-minute 5K runner would gain 18–36 seconds. A 15-minute runner would improve 9–18 seconds.

And it gets better. By running your hard workouts—tempos, hills, drills, and repetitions—in lighter shoes, you'll improve the efficiency of your stride at faster paces. Some runners mistakenly believe that doing hard workouts in heavier shoes strengthens their legs, making race-day running in lighter shoes much easier. Not so. Instead, doing hard workouts in heavy shoes simply hardwires a stride that's slightly different than the one you'll utilize with lighter shoes. The result is a less-efficient stride in the lighter shoe come race day. If your aim is to race fast and efficiently in lighter shoes, then practice running fast and efficiently in lighter shoes.

One caveat to this key: There's a point at which lack of cushioning outweighs the benefit of racing in a lighter flat—and research has shown that barefoot running is the least efficient race choice of all. As a rule of thumb, if your feet hurt due to lack of shoe, add a little more shoe.

Shoe Weight vs. Performance Improvement

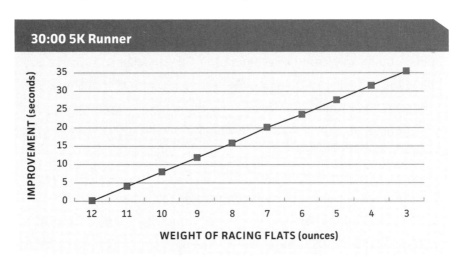

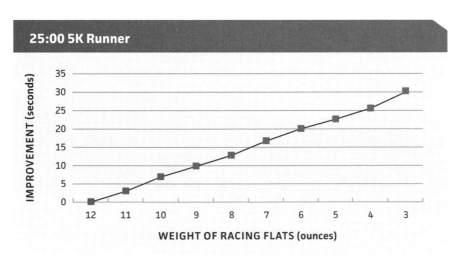

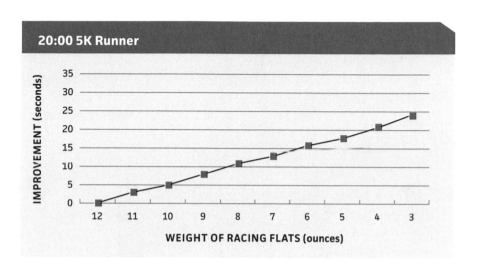

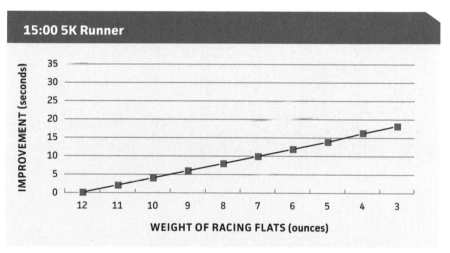

These charts illustrate possible performance improvement for runners of different abilities, based upon the weight of their racing flats. The 12-ounce weight represents the heavy side and assumes the runner is racing in training shoes. The 3-ounce weight represents the light side, and shoes that weigh less than 3 ounces offer no advantage (in fact, studies show there is a disadvantage to shoes lighter than this, as well as to barefoot running).

Sleep, Rest, Recover

This is a simple key that 5K runners can't afford to ignore. You need to recover from training to benefit from training.

That's because you don't get better at running while you're training. You get better while you're recovering.

When you work out, you break down tissue (e.g., muscle, bone, and tendon) and deplete resources like fuel, hormones, and neurotransmitters.

To improve, you'll need to go through two phases of recovery:

Initial repair: You repair damaged tissue and replenish spent resources.

Supercompensation: Following initial repair, your body rebounds from the workout by building even stronger tissues and increasing the volume of your stored resources.

With proper recovery, you end up fitter than you were before training. Without it, you might fail to complete initial recovery, and you won't get the benefit of supercompensation. You won't get fitter. You won't get faster. If you're lucky, you'll merely end up disappointed with your lack of improvement. If you're unlucky, you'll find yourself sick, sore, injured, chronically fatigued, or, worst of all, overtrained. Overtraining syndrome occurs when excessive fatigue and inadequate recovery sends you into a physiological downward spiral—one that can only be arrested by full rest, often extending for a period of two months or more.

Runners sometimes complain, "But I feel good! I'm ready to run hard again." Listen: Feeling good isn't a green light to run hard. You'll "feel good" as soon as you've completed initial repairs, but that doesn't mean you're ready to train hard again. It just means that you're back to where you started. Train hard right away, and you won't improve. Continue to bombard your body with hard workouts, and your body will eventually cry uncle. You'll wonder why all that hard training didn't lead to your 5K

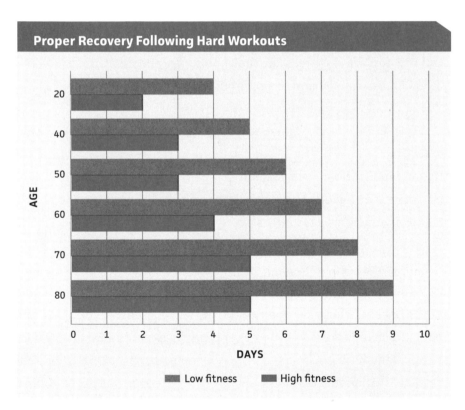

Proper Recovery Following Hard Workouts

This chart offers guidelines for the number of days following a hard workout before runners should perform another hard workout. Note that recovery varies depending on age and fitness.

goal time, and the answer will be that you didn't give all that hard training a chance to work!

To ensure that you recover fully and reap the benefits of supercompensation, follow these guidelines:

1 Within the first 15–30 minutes post-workout, eat a snack that includes at least 50 grams of carbohydrate and 20 grams of protein.

2 Get at least seven hours of sleep per night (elite 5K runners need about nine).

3 Schedule at least 22 hours between workouts—if you're running twice per day, make sure one of the workouts qualifies as "easy," limiting both intensity and volume.

4 Schedule 2–3 days between hard workouts (e.g., repetitions, tempo, hill repeats, etc.).

5 If you're age 40+, consider scheduling 3–5 days between hard workouts.

As a final guideline: Run your hard days hard and your easy days easy. Turning easy runs into "medium" runs recruits more muscle fibers and faster fiber types than required, leading to excess muscle damage and nervous-system fatigue. And performing hard workouts at medium effort leaves you unprepared for the more intense demands of a 5K race.

"Farm when it's sunny, read when it rains." —Japanese saying

Review Non-Running Activities & Hobbies

"One cannot both feast and become rich." —Ashanti proverb

There are runners who plan their entire lives around running.

These runners never miss a workout. They sleep right. Eat right. Never physically overexert themselves at work. They coordinate vacations with races, like the Carlsbad 5000 or the Boston Marathon. And they never participate in activities that put their muscles or connective tissue at risk—no pick-up basketball games at the local YMCA, no bending over to retrieve a quarter from the ground.

I know these runners well because I was one of them.

As a coach, however, I usually work with runners who, for lack of a better description, have a life. They want to run a faster 5K, but that's not all they want. They want to play with their kids. Go on non-running vacations. Help a friend move a refrigerator. Jog up stairs if they're late for a meeting. Coach a local Little League squad. Even bend over for that quarter—or a nickel or a dime.

Which is great and healthy! But it calls to mind an old cliché: You can't have your cake and eat it, too.

I coached a runner via Skype who complained about a tender hamstring after a race. Since I pride myself on injury-prevention, I pressed him on anything he might have done pre- or post-race to put his hammy at risk. He didn't think there was anything—unless it was putting in a new living room floor, mostly while on hands and knees, the previous week, or going straight to a local river post-race to kayak for a few hours. Mystery of the hamstring injury solved.

Often, runner-parents want to combine their own full training schedules with regular "easy" workouts with their kids. Other runners are reluctant to give up weekly, high-intensity CrossFit® or yoga sessions. Some runners work construction or other manual labor jobs. Some enjoy cross-training—biking, swimming, hiking, sailing, skiing, or kayaking. Some have

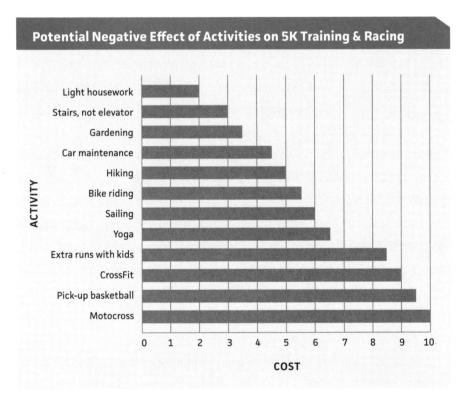

This chart estimates the negative effect of various activities on 5K training and racing. Note that many of the activities with higher scores are safe when worked into your training program, with a proper recovery period scheduled before your next hard running workout.

other strenuous hobbies and activities that are important parts of their lives.

And these are all good things. But just because they're good things doesn't mean they don't count when it comes to balancing out the work-load your body can handle. You only have so much adaptive potential. If you run five miles with your kids' running club, that's five miles of tissue damage and about 500 calories of energy expenditure. A 30-minute session of high-intensity weight training is a hard workout—you'll need two days before your next hard workout. A hard day of manual labor results in stiff, inflamed muscles; you'll have to postpone any hard workout you had scheduled or make do with less intense training.

To run a great 5K, you don't need to insulate yourself from life's experiences. But know that every activity has a cost. A full training schedule for a fast 5K along with a full non-running schedule of hobbies and activities can't coexist. Something has to give. What that "something" is will be determined by you. You'll need to conduct an honest review of your running goals and their importance to you. And then you'll decide how best to balance them with the rest of your life.

One of my favorite quotes comes from science fiction writer Philip K. Dick: "Reality is that which, when you stop believing in it, doesn't go away."

The reality is that your body can only adapt to a limited physical workload each day. Overwhelm it, and you don't get fitter. You break.

PART THREE

RACE-DAY

KEYS

Try a Mini-Taper

"In theory, there is no difference between theory and practice. In practice, there is." —Jan L. A. van de Snepscheut, computer scientist and educator

"I felt great during my workout on Monday, but then I was totally flat for my race on Saturday."

It's a familiar refrain from disappointed 5K racers. They completed their distance runs. Did all their repetitions. Ran hills. Ate right. Slept right. Even did a perfect taper the final week before their race, reducing overall training volume by 40–60 percent.

So what went wrong?

What might have gone wrong was that a traditional taper didn't work for these runners. For some runners, the sudden interruption to their normal training routine doesn't lead to fresh, fit, and fast legs. Instead, it leaves these runners stale, heavy-legged, and, in some cases, susceptible to colds and allergy attacks.

The solution is a mini-taper. Rather than starting your taper 4–7 days out from race day, limit it to the final 2–3 days—with one exception: Eliminate the previous weekend's long run, substituting a regular-length distance run.

During your mini-taper, cut normal volume by 20–25 percent until the day before the race, when you'll limit yourself to 15–30 minutes of easy running. On this final day, younger runners can add 3–4 race pace strides of 40–100 meters. Older runners should consider skipping the strides. While the strides help keep younger legs fresh and ready to

Traditional vs. Mini-Taper for 5K (6-day schedule)		Sun.	Mon.	Tues.	Wed.	Thurs.	Fri.	Sat.
25 miles/ week	Non-taper	OFF	12 × 400m	20 min. distance	6 hill repeats	20 min. distance	20 min. distance	1 hr. long run
	Traditional taper	OFF	6 × 400m	12 min. distance	10 min. & 8–10 strides @ race pace	12 min. distance	12 min. jog, strides @ race pace	5K
	Mini-taper	OFF	12 × 400m	20 min. distance	4 hill repeats	16 min. distance	15 min. jog, strides @ race pace	5K
50 miles/ week	Non-taper	OFF	16 × 400m	1 hr. 15 min. distance	6 hill repeats	1 hr. 15 min. distance	1 hr. 15 min. distance	1 hr. 50 min. long run
	Traditional taper	OFF	8 × 400m	30 min. distance	25 min. & 8–10 strides @ race pace	30 min. distance	20 min. jog, strides @ race pace	5K
	Mini-taper	OFF	16 × 400m	1 hr. 15 min. distance	4 hill repeats	1 hr. distance	20 min. jog, strides @ race pace	5K
75 miles/ week*	Non-taper	OFF	20 × 400m	1 hr. 30 min. distance	6 hill repeats	1 hr. 30 min. distance	1 hr. 30 min. distance	2 hr. 10 min. long run
	Traditional taper	OFF	10 × 400m	35 min. distance	30 min. & 8–10 strides @ race pace	35 min. distance	20 min. jog, strides @ race pace	5K
	Mini-taper	OFF	20 × 400m	1 hr. 30 min. distance	4 hill repeats	1 hr. 10 min. distance	20 min. jog, strides @ race pace	5K

This table compares a non-taper, a traditional taper, and a mini-taper week. Runs are given in time rather than distance.

Note: The mini-taper week is only an example and isn't meant for use as a template.

*For 75-mile weeks, runners need to add extra runs (double workouts) during non-taper and mini-taper weeks, with no extra runs for a traditional taper week.

produce the force required for racing, they can leave the nervous system of older runners slightly fatigued—leading to the exact heavy-legged feeling these runners are trying to avoid.

With a reduced taper, you keep your regular training rhythm and still get enough recovery to ensure full glycogen stores, a refreshed nervous system, and repaired muscle fibers. You might not get the extra boost that accompanies a full taper, but you won't feel like someone super-glued your feet to the start line, either.

Beat the Jitters

"Make sure your worst enemy doesn't live between your own two ears."

—Laird Hamilton, American big-wave surfer

We all get nervous on race day. That's expected.

"Any runner who denies having fears, nerves, or some other kind of disposition," said 1950s British Olympian Gordon Pirie, "is a bad athlete, or a liar."

But for some runners, race jitters (an irrational panic in the buildup to a race) aren't limited to race day. For some, jitters can infect the final weeks before the race. They can lead to unforced errors that upend months of smart training. What makes jitters especially destructive is that runners don't always recognize them, even when they're shaking in their shoes.

Here then, are five common mistakes runners make due to the jitters—along with practical advice for combating them.

1 **Spontaneous injury:** As race day approaches, you suddenly become aware of some acute pain or injury. Your Achilles hurts. Or your back is tight. Or you've got a pain in your hip that you're certain must be a stress fracture. Are you really injured? Yes, you are. Then again, you're always slightly injured. Hard training leads to minor aches and pains. Normally, runners shrug these off— until race anxiety amplifies them in our minds. Don't worry. Once the race starts, you'll forget all about these phantom injuries.

2   **Second-guessing syndrome:** It's the week of your race, and the realization hits: "Everything I've done to prepare for this race is wrong!" You decide you should have done more distance. Or speed. Or tempo. Or drills. You wonder if you should do a crash course in whatever's lacking. Don't. Instead, relax. There's nothing you can do in a week to get faster. At the same time, there's a lot you can do to sabotage your race. Run the race you have in you, then assess afterward whether your training needs a tweak.

3   **Workout warrior:** The race is almost upon you, but you simply can't wait the few remaining days to test your fitness. The solution is clear: Run an all-out time trial or a monster workout . . . No. Just no. Testing your race readiness won't improve your fitness, but it will break down muscle, deplete muscle glycogen, and exhaust your nervous system, leaving you with dead legs on race day. Don't waste your fitness on a workout.

4   **Routine changes:** Some runners change their routine in advance of a race. They think more rest and less exertion will make them a faster runner. So they skip chores. Avoid normal outings. Get more couch time. But operating outside your normal routine only increases anxiety. Instead, stay in your comfort zone. Go to work. Take out the garbage. Eat normally. As über-coach Jack Daniels says, "Most great performances come when you're not trying to do it. When you try to do something special, it usually backfires."

5   **Training through the race:** Sometimes runners decide the best way to deal with race anxiety—about their fitness, training, and race readiness—is to treat the race like a workout. "I don't have

to worry about my performance," the thinking goes, "because I'm just training through the race." Don't do this. A race is a 100 percent effort no matter how you approach it. You need a modest taper prior to race day and a short period of recovery afterward. Otherwise, you risk overloading your body with an effort it can't handle.

Race Week Checklist: Dos & Don'ts
✓ Consider using a mini-taper
✓ Have confidence in your fitness and wait until post-race to assess if any program changes are required
✓ Shorten your long run a week before race day
✓ Take out the garbage
✗ Cancel race if you're not in 100 percent tip-top shape
✗ Carbo-load
✗ Change your diet
✗ Change your training program
✗ Change your work schedule to allow for more rest
✗ Panic over aches and pains
✗ Perform a hard non-running workout or activity the day before the race
✗ Run a monster workout
✗ Test yourself with a time trial
✗ Start a new kickboxing routine
✗ Treat the race like a workout

If there's a common theme to all these jitters, it's this: A lack of confidence in your race-readiness can lead to mistakes that sabotage your race. It's a self-fulfilling prophecy. Instead, trust your training. If the race doesn't go as planned, see Key 25 on post-race assessment.

Race-Day Guidelines (Pre-Race)

Finally, your 5K race day arrives. After months of training, it's time to claim your improved 5K performance. Don't blow it by making silly mistakes.

Rule number one: Arrive early. You're already excited about the race. There's no need to turn excitement into anxiety by arriving late. So allow yourself plenty of time to deal with the usual race-day complications. These can include (but are not limited to):

Traffic jams: Expect highways and streets leading to the race to experience heavy traffic, as all race participants converge on the venue at about the same time.

Parking: Don't assume there will be parking near the race-staging area. Race-adjacent parking tends to fill up fast, and you might end up with a longer walk than you expected.

Registration lines: If bib pickup is on race day, expect a wait. It takes time to log in participants, check IDs, and hand over race bibs, timing chips, and goody bags.

Porta Potty lines: These get longer as the start time draws closer. A short line an hour out becomes a DMV-type line with 15 minutes to go. Race directors rent Porta Potties based on overall attendance— not on demand during the final, frantic minutes pre-race.

Gear change: If you intend to change your shirt, shorts, or shoes between warm-up and race, expect it to take longer than usual. When you get nervous, your fingers don't work very well—a good reason to safety-pin your race bib to your race shirt well in advance.

Start-line positioning: Some race participants forgo the warm-up altogether and make a beeline for the start line. If you're worried about where you'll be standing when the horn goes off, factor extra time at the start line into your warm-up equation.

Rule number two: Speaking of your warm-up, race day is no time to experiment with it. Instead, you'll want to use the exact same warm-up—the same mix of jogging, strides, and dynamic stretching—that you've used during training before hard workouts (and, yes, you should be doing a warm-up before all hard workouts; on pp. 124–125, you'll find specific warm-ups for each type of training).

Your warm-up has a simple physiological purpose: It prepares your muscles, nervous system, endocrine system (i.e., your hormones), and energy systems for the demands of a hard effort. But it also has a more important psychological purpose: It puts you in your comfort zone. As you perform your regular warm-up routine, you experience the familiar sensations that precede your hard workouts. Your muscles lose their stiffness. Your breathing settles down as your aerobic system kicks into gear. Your anxiety about facing a race effort is lessened because you're reminded that your body can handle a hard effort—just as it handles your hard workouts.

Bottom line: Performing your regular warm-up takes the abnormal situation of toeing a race start line with hundreds (or thousands) of runners and makes it feel normal.

Pre-Race Checklist: Dos & Don'ts
✓ Arrive at the race early
✓ Bring a photo ID
✓ Find a place on the start line early
✓ Know where the start and finish lines are located
✓ Use the Porta Potties (or other restroom facilities) early
✗ Alter your warm-up routine for the race
✗ Get flustered if the race is running late
✗ Wait until after your warm-up to attach your timing chip to your shoe

And yes, you'll see scores of runners performing warm-ups that are different from yours. And, yes, some of these runners might be faster than you. That doesn't mean you should change your warm-up to copy theirs. For all you know, they have no idea why they're warming up the way they are—maybe they're copying somebody else. Stick with what you know.

One final piece of advice: Be prepared to stand at the start line beyond the scheduled race start time. With late runner arrivals, speeches by local dignitaries, etc., races often start 10–15 minutes late. Yes, you'll lose some of your warm-up. No, you won't lose all of it. Don't let it fluster you. If you get too frustrated or anxious, it will take its toll during the race.

"Standing on the starting line, we're all cowards." —*Alberto Salazar*

Racing Guidelines

You toe the line for your 5K race. The starting horn sounds. Now what? Now you run a mistake-free race that nets you your 5K goal performance. To accomplish this, you'll want to adhere to a few simple guidelines:

1 **No sprinting off the start line:** While you want to make sure you have good position 400 meters into the race, that doesn't mean sprinting off the start line. Recall from Key 7 that the first 30–40 seconds of the race will be the most anaerobic. The faster you run, the more negative by-products of anaerobic energy production you'll accumulate. That translates to increased fatigue early in the race and a painful slog to the finish. This doesn't mean you should dawdle Get up to race pace quickly. But don't sprint. The laws of physiology don't get suspended just because it's a race.

2 **Don't "bank time":** Some runners try to run the first mile 10–20 seconds faster than goal pace. They think this allows wiggle room later in the race. It doesn't. Running 10–20 seconds faster than 5K pace puts you right on 3K pace. A 3K is a little less than 2 miles. That means you're running a pace you can sustain for less than 2 miles, while thinking you'll somehow stretch your effort to more than 3 miles. You won't. You'll bonk.

3 **No mid-race mini-battles:** There is only one finish line, and it's at the finish. Yes, we've all been there—in the middle of a race, settled into our pace, when suddenly some hard-charging runner edges ahead of us. A primitive fight-or-flight response kicks in, and you think, "No way!" So you fight off the challenge. Congratulations, you just sabotaged your 5K. Accelerating mid-race demands greater muscle-fiber recruitment and an increase in anaerobic energy production. There's a price to pay for that. It's called fatigue.

4 **Draft off other runners:** There's a physiological benefit to running directly behind other runners. By cutting down wind resistance, you decrease the amount of force you must produce. There's also a psychological advantage. Instead of having to focus on pace, you relax and let someone else worry about it. As long as other runners are setting a pace that matches your goal, use them to your advantage.

5 **Run tangents:** The shortest distance between two points is a straight line. If you see that you'll be making a left-hand or right-hand turn up ahead, run a straight line toward that corner (unless your straight line takes you through another runner, in which case you'll need to opt for a slightly modified course). And if you're running through a gradual curve, hug the inside. Just as running in lane two on a track forces you to run farther than in lane one, running wide on a turn adds distance to your race.

6 **You're not alone:** It sometimes seems as if the runners around you look fresher and less stressed than you feel. You start to think

that maybe you're in over your head. You're not. The other runners are just as tired as you. If they weren't, they'd be way ahead of you.

7   **Don't quit when your brain yells, "Quit!":** There will come a time in your 5K when you'll want to quit. You're tired. You hurt. You start to think it isn't your day. Maybe you even think, *If I faked an injury, no one would blame me for stopping.* Don't do it. This is just your brain trying to sabotage your race. Remember what we discussed in Key 13: Your brain is a worrywart. It's sounding a five-alarm warning—fatigue and self-doubt—to get you to give up. Hang in there. Your brain will chill after a minute or two, just in time for you to kick to the finish line.

8   **Target an even effort for your race:** This is probably the most important advice in this book. Run 98 percent of the race, from the start line until the moment you begin your finish sprint, at an even effort. Effort. Not pace. There's a difference.

Even pace: You run each mile (or kilometer) of your race at the same, predetermined pace (e.g., 6-minutes-per-mile). The problem with this approach is twofold. First, terrain, weather, and the presence of other runners makes it hard to do. Second, you simply don't know what the "right" pace will be for race day—guess too fast, and your legs won't last; guess too slow, and you rob yourself of the chance to snag a massive PR.

Even effort: You choose a consistent level of energy expenditure that feels right for race day. You rely on external and internal cues to

Race Checklist: Dos & Don'ts	
✓	Draft off other runners
✓	Race in light racing flats
✓	Remind yourself that those running nearby feel about the same as you and have relatively the same ability
✓	Run at an even effort
✓	Run tangents on the race course
✗	Quit if the race becomes too uncomfortable
✗	Refuse to be passed in the middle of the race
✗	Sprint off the start line

adjust your pace. Your effort won't "feel" the same throughout the 5K. You'll experience increasing fatigue as the race progresses. But you'll burn energy at a consistent rate. To succeed with this approach takes practice, practice, practice. The good news is that a proper training program provides that practice. (One trick I've used for years is to ask myself at intervals throughout a race, "Can I make it to the finish line at this pace?"—it's amazing how accurate the feedback from that simple question can be, if you're willing to take it.)

Implementing the advice in the previous eight guidelines will result in a race that hurts less and gets you to the finish line faster.

"Do. Or do not. There is no try." —*Yoda*

Assess Your Performance

You did it. You completed a 5K race. Maybe you exceeded expectations. Maybe you met them. Maybe you stunk up the joint.

No matter your result, you'll want to assess your performance.

With the help of the Post-Race Assessment, take some time to evaluate your performance as it relates to training, race preparation, and race execution. Then, use what you've learned to better prepare for your next 5K.

First, give yourself time to recover from the race—physically and psychologically—before trying to process the experience. Assessments made in the finish chute, whether negative ("I'm never doing that again!") or positive ("Wow, I was fast!"), often fade after a few hours, or a few days, of reflection—maybe you only hurt during the race due to a racing error, maybe you were fast because the course was a quarter-mile short.

Once you're ready for an objective assessment, target some specific areas of concern.

Base training: Setting aside how you felt about your performance, was your base fitness adequate to complete the race distance?

Race preparation: Did your training prepare you to go the entire 5K distance at your targeted pace/effort, or did the bottom drop out before the race was completed?

Race goal: Was it achievable? If you met it, the answer is, "Yes." If you ran slower, was your goal too aggressive? Or do you feel it's within reach with another race or two?

Race execution: Did you adhere to the race guidelines from Key 24, or did you decide to wing it—and maybe hit a 5K wall at about 3K?

Race choice: Was the race itself a good choice, given your personal goals? If your goal was a time, was the race conducive to a fast pace (e.g., flat with few turns)? If you raced for a challenging experience, did the terrain and competition match your expectations?

Race essentials: How about everything else? How were your shoes? Were your legs springy during the race? How was your overall energy level? Did you arrive early enough, find parking, register, and warm up without having to scramble to the start line?

After assessing your race, remember this: It was just one race. Change things that clearly need changing—like if you ate too big a breakfast and had to make a pit stop during the race—but be patient with everything else.

A few years back, I agreed to coach an athlete, Diana, who'd clocked 23:09 for 5K. She wanted to improve. After three months of training, she entered a 5K. I warned her to expect resistance from her brain— that her brain hadn't raced for several months and would object to the effort. She ran 23:03 and wasn't happy. Two weeks later, she ran 22:11. Two weeks after that, 21:08. Soon, she was down to 20:22. Diana's race times dropped at an astounding rate. But it wasn't a case of her fitness improving. Remember, physical changes occur incrementally. Instead,

Post-Race Assessment

Question	✓	✗
Did my training improve my overall fitness (from previous races)? *What changes can I make?*	✓	✗
Did my training prepare me to cover my 5K race at goal pace/effort? *What changes can I make?*	✓	✗
Was my pre-race goal achievable? *What changes can I make?*	✓	✗
Did I arrive early enough for the race? *What changes can I make?*	✓	✗
Were my legs fresh, bouncy, and ready to race? *What changes can I make?*	✓	✗
Was my overall energy level good at the race start? *What changes can I make?*	✓	✗
Was my overall energy level adequate for the entire race? *What changes can I make?*	✓	✗
Was the race terrain conducive to a fast 5K? *What changes can I make?*	✓	✗
Was I mentally prepared for the stress of the race? *What changes can I make?*	✓	✗
Did I follow my race plan? *What changes can I make?*	✓	✗
Did I use other runners to my benefit? *What changes can I make?*	✓	✗
Do I need to train race pace/effort with other runners in order to be more comfortable during a race? *What changes can I make?*	✓	✗
Was my pre-race meal adequate? *What changes can I make?*	✓	✗
Was my outfit compatible with weather conditions? *What changes can I make?*	✓	✗
Did my shoes help or hinder my performance? *What changes can I make?*	✓	✗
Overall, am I satisfied with my race? *What changes can I make?*	✓	✗
Based on this race, what is my next race goal? *What changes can I make?*	✓	✗

Diana's brain had gradually accepted that a faster 5K wasn't going to kill her. Her brain allowed her to access the physiological adaptations she'd earned with her training.

So train properly. And race smart. And assess your fitness and performance, the better to train and race well in the future. But be patient, too.

The 25 keys in this book will help you run a faster 5K, but the advice is only as good as your willingness to take it. There are effective training, lifestyle, and race execution adjustments you can make to absolutely become a better 5K runner. But there are no shortcuts. That's what I love about our sport. When we train better, we get fitter, and we race faster. There is no luck in running—no hitting a one-in-a-million full-court swish with a basketball. By training and living correctly, we earn every result.

"The only real mistake is the one from which we learn nothing."

—*John Powell, Jesuit priest and author*

Age-Related Adjustments & Advice

Masters runners sometimes ask me why my books and magazine articles offer so little in the way of masters-specific training adjustments and advice.

The answer is simple. There are no super-secret adjustments or workouts for masters runners. We have to do the same training as younger runners—just a little less of it, at a slightly reduced intensity, with a little more time between hard workouts.

I've love to tell you that "age is just a number" or that "you're only as old as you feel," but the reality is that masters undergo physiological changes that must be acknowledged. As a masters runner, I've set American 5K records for age groups 45–49, 50–54, and 55–59. But the difference between my age 45 record and my age 55 record is more than a minute (hint: I got slower, not faster). This isn't meant to discourage you. On the contrary, I felt wonderful running all of those records. But I only succeeded because I adjusted my training to the realities of aging.

Several things happen to our running bodies as we age:

- Our VO$_2$max decreases.
- We lose faster (fast-twitch and intermediate) muscle fibers.
- We suffer decreased mobility in our hips and ankles.
- Our connective tissue (bones, tendons, ligaments, and cartilage) becomes less supple and more fragile.

- Our nervous system performs less efficiently.
- Our bodies take longer to heal and require additional recovery between workouts.

I call masters training a "no-mistake zone." If we make a single mistake—if we run a repetition workout too hard, or sleep too little before a long run, or shortchange our warm-up before a race—we pay for it. And payment usually takes the form of injury, illness, burnout, or, at a minimum, substandard performance.

On the other hand, if you train correctly and perform every workout (and recovery) by the book, you can expect to achieve top fitness and run a remarkable 5K.

With that faster 5K in mind, here are some masters guidelines you'll want to consider:

No junk miles: Overall mileage is still important, but that doesn't mean you should squeeze extra distance into workouts. No 3-mile cooldown runs after hard workouts; 5–10 minutes will do the trick. No extending distance runs a mile or two to hit arbitrary weekly totals—like shooting for 50 miles instead of 49. And sorry, no long feel-good runs immediately post-race; your body needs recovery, not celebratory miles.

Skip the final repetition: Masters legend Nolan Shaheed (4:25 mile at age 51 and 4:53 at age 62) once told me, "I always skip the final repetition of an intervals workout—that's the one that injures you." Early in a workout, your muscles absorb most of the impact force that occurs with each foot strike. But as your muscles fatigue, more and more of that impact force gets transferred to your connective tissue.

Tired muscles and overstressed connective tissue make those final repetitions a minefield for injury. Obviously, it doesn't work to say you're going to run a certain number of reps while knowing you'll do less. The real point is this: End a hard workout while your legs are still feeling strong.

Train only as hard as required: You have a limited ability to adapt from any single workout. When you run harder than required to stimulate the desired adaptation, you increase the time it takes to recover and elevate your risk of injury. While this is good advice for runners of all ages, it should be a rule for masters runners.

Recover, recover, recover: You don't get fit while you're training; you get fit while you're recovering. Review Key 19 if you need a refresher course on this concept. Between hard workouts, you need time to recover from the first workout and then to supercompensate. Most masters athletes in their 40s can get by with 2–3 days between hard outings (no more than 2–3 hard outings per week). Runners a decade or two—or three or four—older might manage only a single hard workout per week. Bottom line: Don't run your next hard workout until you've recovered from the previous one.

Pick your races: I have masters friends who race every weekend. More power to them! But if you're like me, that's a recipe for injury, burnout, and poor performance. As older runners, many of us need to limit our total races. Since masters runners require a minimum of a week to recover from a 5K (more for longer races), weekly races curtail the amount of hard training we can perform, which in turn limits the opportunity to improve our fitness and run faster. And because races are 100 percent efforts, racing every weekend eventually becomes a load that our bodies can't handle. We get slower. Races feel harder. And we begin to wonder if, in the words of Roger Murtaugh (played by Danny Glover) from the film *Lethal Weapon*, we're "getting too old for this sh#t."

Limit the crosstraining: If your goal is all-around fitness, then crosstrain. But if your goal is a faster 5K, most cross won't help. I can hear the howls of outrage. We oldsters are constantly told that we must crosstrain—as if getting older suddenly imbues crosstraining with a magic that eludes younger runners. There's a physiological principle called "specificity of training." It requires that an athlete—young or old—train their muscle fibers, nervous system, and energy systems in the exact way they'll be used during competition. So while riding a bike improves your cycling, it doesn't make you a better runner. You'll get some benefit from limited crosstraining—we've discussed the benefits of resistance training, and the elliptical machine and ElliptiGO bike are great options when you're injured—but that doesn't justify setting aside a large percentage of your training time and energy for non-running-specific exercise.

Embrace age-grading: Age-grading scores your 5K result (as well as results from other race distances) as a percentage of the maximum expected performance for your age. Given that we all slow down as we age, this offers a way to track your age-adjusted performance from one year to the next—or to compare your current time against times from years past. You can find these calculators online.

As a masters runner, I've competed in track, cross-country, and road racing. I've set records from 1500 meters to the half-marathon. But if pressed to name my favorite race, it would be the 5K. Training for the 5K has it all: distance, drills, hills, tempo, repetitions, sprints, resistance training, and more. Racing the 5K challenges every aspect of our fitness: endurance, speed, strength, and race discipline. Best of all, post-5K, we recover quickly. We can get right back to training and planning our next race. Honestly, masters racing doesn't get any better than that.

"I've learned that it's what you do with the miles, rather than how many you've run." —Rod DeHaven, American Olympic marathoner

WORKOUTS & TRAINING PLANS

Warm-Up Routines

TYPE OF WARM-UP	Jogging/ easy running	Stretching
Resistance training	10–15 min. (optional) or distance run (optional)	N/A
Technique drills	12–15 min.	N/A
Distance	N/A	N/A
Tempo repeats	10–15 min.	N/A
VO$_2$max reps	12–15 min.	Limited dynamic stretching (1–3 stretches, 2–5 min. total), such as leg swings, skipping drill, flat-footed marching drill, butt kick drill (optional)
Short reps	10–15 min.	Limited dynamic stretching, such as leg swings, skipping drill, flat-footed marching drill, butt kick drill (optional, see notes)
Hill repeats	12–15 min.	N/A
Downhill running	12–15 min.	N/A
Goal pace reps— competition warm-up	12–20 min.	Limited dynamic stretching, such as leg swings, skipping drill, flat-footed marching drill, butt kick drill (optional)
5K Race— competition warm-up	12–20 min.	Limited dynamic stretching, such as leg swings, skipping drill, flat-footed marching drill, butt kick drill (optional)

Strides	Short strides	Notes
N/A	N/A	*A running warm-up isn't required, but do 1 set of easy air squats or 1–2 sets of easy (i.e., light) reps with weight at the beginning of your session. If performing multiple sets of each exercise, make the first set lighter than the others.*
2–4 × 60–80m, with equal distance jog recovery	N/A	*N/A*
N/A	N/A	*N/A*
2–4 × 15–20 sec. tempo-paced stride (optional)	N/A	*N/A*
4 × 100m strides (at rep pace), with equal distance jog recovery or 4 × 20 sec. (at rep pace), with 40 sec. jog recovery	N/A	*If you're running these on a track, include dynamic stretching. If you're running on road or trail, skip it. Don't do a lot of dynamic stretching, as you want to limit the time interval between jogging and strides (and also because doing more is counterproductive).*
On roads: 2–4 × 10–15 sec. strides at short rep workout pace or on track: use competition warm-up recommendations (see below)	N/A	*If you're running these on a track, include dynamic stretching. If you're running on road or trail, skip it.*
4–6 × 10–20 sec. strides, with equal distance jog recovery	N/A	*N/A*
4–6 × 10–20 sec. strides, with equal distance jog recovery	N/A	*Do strides on level terrain, limiting downhill running to the workout.*
4 × 100m strides (at rep pace), with equal distance jog recovery or 4 × 20 sec. (at rep pace), with 40 sec. jog recovery	1–4 × 20–40m quick strides (slightly faster than rep pace), with a walk of equal distance for recovery	*A few quick strides at the start line can help prepare the legs for the workout. Make sure to finish these at least 2 min. before starting reps.*
4 × 100m strides (at race pace), with equal distance jog recovery or 4 × 20 sec. (at race pace), with 40 sec. jog recovery	1–4 × 20–40m quick strides (slightly faster than race pace), with a walk of equal distance for recovery	*A few quick strides at the start line can help prepare the legs for a race. Make sure to finish this warm-up at least 2 min. before race start.*

Length of Distance Runs (Distance Runs-Only Schedule)

WEEKLY MILEAGE	NUMBER OF TRAINING DAYS PER WEEK									
	3 DAYS		4 DAYS		5 DAYS		6 DAYS		7 DAYS	
	Distance runs	Long run	Distance runs	Long run	Distance runs	Long run	Distance runs	Long run	Distance runs	Long run
10	3	4–5	3	No long run						
15	3–4	5–6	3	5–6	3	4–5				
20	5–6	8–9	4–5	6–7	3–4	5–6	3	4–5		
25	7–8	10–11	5–6	8–9	4–5	6–7	3–4	6–7	3–4	5
30	8–9	12–13	6–7	10–11	5–6	8–9	4–5	6–7	3–4	6–7
35	8–9 (+5)	12–13	7–8	11–12	6–7	9–10	5–6	8–9	4–5	6–7
40	8–9 (+10)	12–13	8–9	12–13	7–8	10–11	6–7	9–10	5–6	7–8
45			9–10	14–15	8–9	12–13	6–7	10–11	6–7	8–9
50			9–10 (+5)	14–15	9–10	13–14	7–8	11–12	6–7	9–10
55			9–10 (+10)	14–15	9–10	14–15	8–9	12–13	7–8	10–11
60					10–11 (+3)	14–15	9–10	13–14	8–9	11–12
65					10–11 (+8)	14–15	9–10	14–15	8–9	12–13
70					10–11 (+13)	14–15	10–11	14–15	9–10	13–14
75							10–11 (+5)	14–15	9–10	14–15
80							10–11 (+10)	14–15	10–11	14–15

Note: Wondering how many miles each run should be? This table breaks down the required distance for each of your runs. It does not factor in hard workouts (e.g., VO₂max reps, hill repeats). To include those, keep track of a workout's total mileage, then distribute or subtract the difference in mileage over the rest of the week. Blank cells indicate there isn't a safe or effective combination of runs for that mileage/days-per-week combination. To use the table, find your weekly mileage goal on the left, then scan right to find the suggested distance for your runs based on the number of days/week you will train. Numbers in parentheses indicate the amount of extra weekly mileage required to hit your goal; you'll need to lower your mileage goal, add more training days, or add second runs. (Note: Second runs are done in the a.m. or p.m. of days you're already running. They should be 3–5 miles, run at an easy/recovery pace.)

Length of Distance Runs (Competitive Plan) (2 hard workouts per week)

WEEKLY MILEAGE	NUMBER OF TRAINING DAYS PER WEEK								
	3 DAYS	4 DAYS		5 DAYS		6 DAYS		7 DAYS	
	Long run	1 distance run	Long run	2 distance runs	Long run	3 distance runs	Long run	4 distance runs	Long run
20	7–8	3	4–5						
25	12–13	4–5	7–8	3–4	5–6				
30	13 (+5)	6–7	10–11	4–5	7–8	4–5	6–7		
35	13 (+10)	9–10	12–13	6–7	9–10	4–5	7–8	3–4	6–7
40		10 (+3)	13–14	7–8	10–12	5–6	9–10	4–5	7–8
45		10 (+7)	14–15	9–10	13–14	6–7	11–12	5–6	8–9
50		10 (+12)	14–15	10 (+3)	13–14	7–8	12–13	6–7	9–10
55				10 (+7)	14–15	9–10	13–14	7–8	10–11
60				10 (+12)	14–15	10 (+3)	13–14	8–9	13–14
65				10 (+17)	14–15	10 (+7)	14–15	9–10	13–14
70						10 (+12)	14–15	10 (+3)	13–14
75						10 (+17)	14–15	10 (+7)	14–15
80								10 (+12)	14–15
85								10 (+17)	14 15
90								11 (+18)	14–15
95								11 (+22)	14–15

Note: Wondering how many miles to run on non-hard workout days? If you're a competitive runner who includes two hard workouts (e.g. VO$_2$max reps, hill repeats, tempo) in your weekly training program, then this table is your guide. Blank cells indicate there isn't a safe or effective combination of runs for that mileage/days-per-week combination. To use the table, find your weekly mileage goal on the left, then scan right to find the suggested distance for your runs based on the number of days/week you will train. Numbers in parentheses indicate the amount of extra weekly mileage required to hit your mileage goal; you'll need to lower your mileage goal, add more training days, or add second runs. (Note: second runs are done in the a.m. or p.m. of days you are already running. They should be 3–5 miles at an easy/recovery pace.)

Training Paces

5K RACE TIME	Easy/recovery distance pace (per mile)	Distance pace (per mile)	Half-marathon tempo pace (per mile)	60-minute tempo pace (per mile)
14:00	6:35–7:55	5:55–6:55	5:00–5:05	4:50–4:58
14:30	6:45–8:10	6:10–7:05	5:10–5:15	4:58–5:06
15:00	7:00–8:25	6:20–7:20	5:20–5:25	5:14–5:22
15:30	7:15–8:40	6:30–7:35	5:30–5:35	5:22–5:30
16:00	7:25–8:55	6:45–7:45	5:40–5:45	5:30–5:38
16:30	7:40–9:10	6:55–8:00	5:50–5:55	5:38–5:46
17:00	7:50–9:25	7:05–8:15	5:55–6:00	5:46–5:54
17:30	8:05–9:40	7:20–8:25	6:05–6:10	6:02–6:10
18:00	8:15–9:55	7:30–8:40	6:15–6:20	6:10–6:18
18:30	8:30–10:10	7:40–8:55	6:25–6:30	6:18–6:26
19:00	8:40–10:25	7:55–9:05	6:35–6:40	6:26–6:34
19:30	8:55–10:40	8:05–9:20	6:45–6:50	6:34–6:42
20:00	9:10–10:55	8:15–9:35	6:55–7:00	6:42–6:50
20:30	9:20–11:10	8:30–9:45	7:05–7:10	6:58–7:06
21:00	9:35–11:25	8:40–10:00	7:15–7:20	7:06–7:15
21:30	9:45–11:40	8:50–10:15	7:25–7:30	7:15–7:23
22:00	10:00–11:55	9:05–10:25	7:35–7:40	7:23–7:31
22:30	10:10–12:10	9:15–10:40	7:45–7:50	7:39–7:47
23:00	10:25–12:25	9:25–10:55	7:55–8:00	7:47–7:55
23:30	10:40–12:40	9:40–11:05	8:05–8:10	7:55–8:03
24:00	10:50–12:55	9:50–11:20	8:15–8:20	8:03–8:11
24:30	11:05–13:10	10:00–11:35	8:25–8:30	8:11–8:19
25:00	11:15–13:25	10:05–11:35	8:35–8:40	8:19–8:27
25:30	11:25–13:40	10:10–11:35	8:45–8:50	8:35–8:43
26:00	11:40–13:50	10:25–11:45	8:50–8:55	8:43–8:51
26:30	11:50–14:05	10:35–12:00	9:00–9:05	8:51–8:59
27:00	12:00–14:15	10:45–12:10	9:10–9:15	8:59–9:07
27:30	12:15–14:30	10:55–12:25	9:20–9:25	9:07–9:15
28:00	12:25–14:40	11:10–12:35	9:30–9:35	9:23–9:31
28:30	12:35–14:55	11:20–12:50	9:40–9:45	9:31–9:39

10K pace (per mile)	5K pace (per mile)	5K pace (per 400m)	3K pace (per 400m)	Mile/1500 pace (per 400m)
4:34–4:42	4:26–4:34	1:06–1:08	1:04–1:06	1:01–1:02
4:50–4:58	4:34–4:42	1:08–1:10	1:06–1:08	1:02–1:04
4:58–5:06	4:50–4:50	1:12–1:12	1:08–1:10	1:04–1:06
5:06–5:14	4:58–5:06	1:14–1:16	1:12–1:14	1:06–1:08
5:14–5:22	5:06–5:14	1:16–1:18	1:14–1:16	1:08–1:10
5:30–5:38	5:14–5:22	1:18–1:20	1:16–1:18	1:10–1:12
5:38–5:46	5:22–5:30	1:20–1:22	1:18–1:20	1:14–1:16
5:46–5:54	5:38–5:38	1:24–1:24	1:20–1:22	1:16–1:18
5:54–6:02	5:46–5:54	1:26–1:28	1:22–1:24	1:18–1:20
6:10–6:18	5:54–6:02	1:28–1:30	1:26–1:28	1:20–1:22
6:18–6:26	6:02–6:10	1:30–1:32	1:28–1:30	1:22–1:24
6:26–6:34	6:10–6:18	1:32–1:34	1:30–1:32	1:24–1:26
6:34–6:42	6:26–6:26	1:36–1:36	1:32–1:34	1:26–1:28
6:50–6:58	6:34–6:42	1:38–1:40	1:34–1:36	1:28–1:30
6:58–7:06	6:42–6:50	1:40–1:42	1:36–1:38	1:30–1:32
7:06–7:15	6:50–6:58	1:42–1:44	1:40–1:42	1:32–1:34
7:15–7:23	6:58–7:06	1:44–1:46	1:42–1:44	1:34–1:36
7:31–7:39	7:15–7:15	1:48–1:48	1:44–1:46	1:38–1:40
7:39–7:47	7:23–7:31	1:50–1:52	1:46–1:48	1:40–1:42
7:47–7:55	7:31–7:39	1:52–1:54	1:48–1:50	1:42–1:44
7:55–8:03	7:39–7:47	1:54–1:56	1:50–1:52	1:44–1:47
8:11–8:19	7:47–7:55	1:56–1:58	1:54–1:56	1:46–1:48
8:19–8:27	8:03–8:03	2:00–2:00	1:56–1:58	1:48–1:50
8:27–8:35	8:11–8:19	2:02–2:04	1:58–2:00	1:50–1:52
8:35–8:43	8:19–8:27	2:04–2:06	2:00–2:02	1:52–1:54
8:51–8:59	8:27–8:35	2:06–2:08	2:02–2:04	1:54–1:56
8:59–9:07	8:35–8:43	2:08–2:10	2:04–2:06	1:56–1:58
9:07–9:15	8:51–8:51	2:12–2:12	2:08–2:10	1:58–2:00
9:15–9:23	8:59–9:07	2:14–2:16	2:10–2:12	2:00–2:02
9:31–9:39	9:07–9:15	2:16–2:18	2:12–2:14	2:04–2:06

>

5K RACE TIME	Easy/recovery distance pace (per mile)	Distance pace (per mile)	Half-marathon tempo pace (per mile)	60-minute tempo pace (per mile)
29:00	12:45–15:05	11:30–13:00	9:50–9:55	9:39–9:47
29:30	13:00–15:20	11:40–13:15	9:55–10:00	9:47–9:55
30:00	13:10–15:30	11:55–13:25	10:05–10:10	9:55–10:04
30:30	13:20–15:45	12:05–13:35	10:15–10:20	10:12–10:20
31:00	13:30–15:55	12:15–13:50	10:25–10:30	10:20–10:28
31:30	13:45–16:10	12:30–14:00	10:35–10:40	10:28–10:36
32:00	13:55–16:20	12:40–14:15	10:45–10:50	10:36–10:44
32:30	14:05–16:35	12:50–14:25	10:55–11:00	10:44–10:52
33:00	14:15–16:45	13:00–14:40	11:05–11:10	10:52–11:00
33:30	14:30–16:55	13:15–14:50	11:10–11:15	11:08–11:16
34:00	14:40–17:10	13:25–15:05	11:20–11:25	11:16–11:24
34:30	14:50–17:20	13:35–15:15	11:30–11:35	11:24–11:32
35:00	15:00–17:35	13:45–15:30	11:40–11:45	11:32–11:40
35:30	15:15–17:45	14:00–15:40	11:50–11:55	11:40–11:48
36:00	15:25–18:00	14:10–15:55	12:00–12:05	11:56–12:04
36:30	15:35–18:10	14:20–16:05	12:10–12:15	12:04–12:12
37:00	15:45–18:25	14:30–16:20	12:15–12:20	12:12–12:20
37:30	16:00–18:35	14:45–16:30	12:25–12:30	12:20–12:28
38:00	16:10–18:50	14:55–16:45	12:35–12:40	12:28–12:36
38:30	16:20–19:00	15:05–16:55	12:45–12:50	12:44–12:52
39:00	16:35–19:15	15:15–17:10	12:55–13:00	12:52–13:01
39:30	16:45–19:25	15:30–17:20	13:05–13:10	13:01–13:09
40:00*	16:55–19:40	15:40–17:35	13:15–13:20	13:09–13:17
40:30*	17:05–19:50	15:50–17:45	13:20–13:25	13:17–13:25
41:00*	17:20–20:05	16:05–17:55	13:30–13:35	13:33–13:41
41:30*	17:30–20:15	16:15–18:10	13:40–13:45	13:41–13:49
42:00*	17:40–20:30	16:25–18:20	13:50–13:55	13:49–13:57
42:30*	17:50–20:40	16:35–18:35	14:00–14:05	13:57–14:05
43:00*	18:05–20:55	16:50–18:45	14:10–14:15	14:05–14:13
43:30*	18:15–21:05	17:00–19:00	14:20–14:25	14:21–14:29

10K pace (per mile)	5K pace (per mile)	5K pace (per 400m)	3K pace (per 400m)	Mile/1500 pace (per 400m)
9:39–9:47	9:15–9:23	2:18–2:20	2:14–2:16	2:06–2:08
9:47–9:55	9:23–9:31	2:20–2:22	2:16–2:18	2:08–2:10
9:55–10:04	9:39–9:39	2:24–2:24	2:18–2:20	2:10–2:12
10:12–10:20	9:47–9:55	2:26–2:28	2:22–2:24	2:12–2:14
10:20–10:28	9:55–10:04	2:28–2:30	2:24–2:26	2:14–2:16
10:28–10:36	10:04–10:12	2:30–2:32	2:26–2:28	2:16–2:18
10:36–10:44	10:12–10:20	2:32–2:34	2:28–2:30	2:18–2:20
10:52–11:00	10:28–10:28	2:36–2:36	2:30–2:32	2:20–2:22
11:00–11:08	10:36–10:44	2:38–2:40	2:32–2:34	2:22–2:24
11:08–11:16	10:44–10:52	2:40–2:42	2:36–2:38	2:24–2:26
11:16–11:24	10:52–11:00	2:42–2:44	2:38–2:40	2:28–2:30
11:32–11:40	11:00–11:08	2:44–2:46	2:40–2:42	2:30–2:32
11:40–11:48	11:16–11:16	2:48–2:48	2:42–2:44	2:32–2:34
11:48–11:56	11:24–11:32	2:50–2:52	2:44–2:46	2:34–2:36
11:56–12:04	11:32–11:40	2:52–2:54	2:46–2:48	2:36–2:38
12:12–12:20	11:40–11:48	2:54–2:56	2:50–2:52	2:38–2:40
12:20–12:28	11:48–11:56	2:56–2:58	2:52–2:54	2:40–2:42
12:28–12:36	12:04–12:04	3:00–3:00	2:54–2:56	2:42–2:44
12:36–12:44	12:12–12:20	3:02–3:04	2:56–2:58	2:44–2:46
12:52–13:01	12:20–12:28	3:04–3:06	2:58–3:00	2:46–2:48
13:01–13:09	12:28–12:36	3:06–3:08	3:00–3:02	2:48–2:50
13:09–13:17	12:36–12:44	3:08–3:10	3:04–3:06	2:52–2:54
13:17–13:25	12:52–12:52	3:12–3:12	3:06–3:08	2:54–2:56
13:33–13:41	13:01–13:09	3:14–3:16	3:08–3:10	2:56–2:58
13:41–13:49	13:09–13:17	3:16–3:18	3:10–3:12	2:58–3:00
13:49–13:57	13:17–13:25	3:18–3:20	3:12–3:14	3:00–3:02
13:57–14:05	13:25–13:33	3:20–3:22	3:14–3:16	3:02–3:04
14:13–14:21	13:41–13:41	3:24–3:24	3:18–3:20	3:04–3:06
14:21–14:29	13:49–13:57	3:26–3:28	3:20–3:22	3:06–3:08
14:29–14:37	13:57–14:05	3:28–3:30	3:22–3:24	3:08–3:10

>

5K RACE TIME	Easy/recovery distance pace (per mile)	Distance pace (per mile)	Half-marathon tempo pace (per mile)	60-minute tempo pace (per mile)
44:00*	18:25–21:15	17:10–19:10	14:30–14:35	14:29–14:37
44:30*	18:35–21:30	17:20–19:25	14:35–14:40	14:37–14:45
45:00*	18:50–21:40	17:35–19:35	14:45–14:50	14:45–14:53

Note: Recommended paces are given as a range. Fit runners should target the faster end of the range; beginner runners or those struggling with the faster pace can target the slower end of the range.

*Runners with a 5K time of 40 min.+ may require training-pace adjustments, such as: 1) Opt for walk/jog workouts in place of distance runs until fitness/running pace improves; 2) Run both tempo and VO₂max work at 5K pace, since 5K pace often represents only a slight increase in pace over normal distance runs; 3) Speed up distance paces if the table's listed running pace isn't comfortable for you.

10K pace (per mile)	5K pace (per mile)	5K pace (per 400m)	3K pace (per 400m)	Mile/1500 pace (per 400m)
14:37–14:45	14:05–14:15	3:30–3:32	3:24–3:26	3:10–3:12
14:52–15:01	14:13–14:21	3:32–3:34	3:26–3:28	3:12–3:14
15:01–15:09	14:29–14:29	3:36–3:36	3:28–3:30	3:16–3:18

Training Schedules

This book offers you four training plans to choose from:

1. **Beginner's 12-Week Plan (plus 3 weeks base training):** This plan is for new runners and those returning to the sport after a long absence. Some readers won't be ready to run on day one, so the plan offers three weeks of base training, during which your muscles, connective tissue, aerobic system, and nervous system will be prepared for the challenge of training. This plan is aggressive and assumes runners are focused on running a fast 5K.

2. **12-Week Plan (plus 1 week base training):** This plan is for experienced athletes who are currently engaged in an exercise program, whether that is at least three days of running per week or a similar schedule of activities such as soccer, cycling, basketball, or aerobics.

3. **16-Week Extended Plan (plus 1 week base training):** This plan includes training from all 15 training keys and is very aggressive.

4. **12-Week Low-Intensity Plan:** This plan allows runners to craft their own program—whether this is because of a preference for a more distance-oriented schedule, a lack of appropriate facilities (e.g., a track, trail, or hills), or to complement a custom-tailored schedule. The program suggests one Monday workout

per week and offers advice for other days, but consider it a "Mr. Potato Head," where you pick the variation you like, for the self-coached runner.

Most plans include 1 week of extra **base training** (i.e., one more week of preparatory training for runners with limited fitness backgrounds). Runners who are already including reps (or even strides) in their programs won't need this, but runners who've focused strictly on distance will want to prep their legs for varied pace work. As for **frequency**, all 12-week plans are formatted for runners scheduling 3–7 days of running per week. The 16-week extended plan requires runners to schedule a minimum of 4 days of running per week, with the option of running up to 7 days per week. Finally, every plan allows runners to choose their number of training days per week, mileage, and paces for workouts. To get the most out of your training, refer to these tables:

▸ **Warm-Up Routines (page 124):** It's important to warm up before hard workouts. This table couples various workouts with a suggested warm-up.

▸ **Length of Distance Runs (page 126):** These two tables split your weekly mileage into "distance runs" and "long runs." The first table assumes an all-distance schedule, with no "hard" workouts—but you can add hard workouts to your schedule by calculating the mileage for those workouts and then adjusting the week's remaining runs. The second table is for use with the training schedules and factors in the mileage required to perform two hard workouts each week. Both tables help you pick the proper length for your runs.

▸ **Training Paces (page 128):** Find your current 5K pace in the left-hand column, then use the training paces in the targeted row. If you don't know your 5K pace, either guesstimate a time or guesstimate training effort during your workouts.

Basic Rules for All Plans

1 **Follow workouts in the order they're presented:** Workouts create changes in your body that are required to run future workouts and to reinforce past ones. Changing the order (or the workout) sabotages both the work you've done and the work you'll do.

2 **Stick to prescribed paces:** The pace prescribed for a workout isn't about time; it's about the muscle fibers, energy systems, and nervous-system recruitment represented by that pace. Running faster or slower changes the workout. If you were mailing a package from Florida to Texas, and your delivery service proudly announced they'd shipped the package all the way to California, you wouldn't thank them for shipping it farther than requested. Same for running your workouts too hard.

3 **Don't skimp on recovery:** You can alter the schedules so that hard days and long runs better match your personal schedule, but do not eliminate recovery between hard sessions in order to make that happen. Running two hard days in a row is a program killer.

4   **Your success is a product of your training:** Athletes sometimes
    ask me if they can find the same success running 3–4 days a week
    as running 6–7 days a week. The answer is simple: no. As long as
    you train smart, balancing hard work and recovery, you'll see
    better results by running more. Coaches, books, or articles that
    promise you differently are lying. You can get fit on 3–4 days per
    week. But runners who can handle higher volume (not everyone
    can) will get fitter on 5 days. More so on 6 or 7 days. Decide
    what's right for your schedule and goals. And be honest about
    how much training your body can absorb; part of what makes
    some runners "elite" is that their bodies can absorb a workload
    that would injure mere mortals. But at the end of the day, your
    5K will be a product of your training. So choose wisely.

READY, SET, GO!

Beginner's 12-Week Plan

(plus 3 weeks extra base training)

This plan is for those training 3–5 days per week and does not include specific days for a post-run stretching and exercise routine or an injury-prevention and resistance training routine (see Key 14). The former routine can be scheduled for any day of the week, though regular distance-run days are advised. The latter routine should not be combined with a Monday or Wednesday hard workout.

	Sunday	Monday	Tuesday	Wednesday
BASE TRAINING I	OFF	Walk: 15–30 min. *As the expression goes: "Walk before you run." Walking strengthens muscles and connective tissue. So when you do run, you'll be ready for it.*	OFF	Walk: 15–30 min. *DOMS (delayed onset muscle soreness) tends to peak 48 hours after exercise. If you're sore today, it may mean you walked too fast or too far on Monday. If that's the case, walk a little less or a little slower today. If the pain is really bad, take the day off.*
BASE TRAINING II	OFF	Walk/jog 20–30 min. First 5 min. are walking only. Include 10 × 30 sec. jogging surges, with at least a minute of walking between surges. *Jogging is low effort. You should be 100% comfortable during surges. Do not push it!*	OFF	Walk: 15–60 min. *No jogging today. Instead, extend your walk if your legs are feeling good.*
BASE TRAINING III	OFF	Walk/run easy 30–40 min. First 5 min. are walking only. Include 5–10 × 2 min. easy running surges, with 1 min. walking between surges. Walk for remaining min. *Increase effort slightly from jogging, but you shouldn't be breathing hard or in pain. Do as many reps as you feel comfortable with.*	OFF	Walk/run easy 30–40 min. First 5 min. are walking only. Include 8–10 × 2 min. easy running surges, with 1 min. of walking between surges. Walk for remaining min. *Complete at least 8 reps. If you're sore or tired, you may have run too hard on Monday. Slow down the pace today.*

Runners who want to race before Week 12 should use the 2-Week Adjustment schedule at the end of this schedule (not the adjustment on pp. 174–175). It's recommended that you complete at least the first six weeks of this schedule before planning a race.

Thursday	Friday	Saturday	Weekly thoughts
OFF	Walk: 15–30 min. *Stick with walking. You want your body to adapt to an entire week of walking. You can expect fortified muscles for your first jogging next Mon.*	OFF or 15–30 min. walking *If you will stick to a 3-days-per-week schedule, skip this day. Otherwise, go for a walk to help establish your new training routine.*	*The base training phase is for runners who haven't been engaging in physical exercise before starting this 5K program. If you've already been doing a combination of walking, jogging, or running, move straight to Week 1 of the schedule.*
OFF	Walk/jog 30–40 min. First 5 min. are walking only. Include 10 × 1 min. jogging surges, with at least 1 min. walking between surges. *Be patient. In a little over a week you'll be doing a continuous distance run.*	OFF or 15–60 min. walking *Two jogging sessions for this week are enough. Enjoy this walk.*	*Remember, don't turn "jogging" into "running" (or sprinting) at this stage. The most destructive saying in fitness is, "No pain, no gain." On the contrary, if your training is painful at this point, you're doing it wrong.*
OFF	Walk/run easy 35–40 min. First 5 min. are walking only. Include 10 × 2 min. easy running surges, with 1 min. walking between surges. Walk for remaining min. *10 reps equals 20 min. of running, the length of Monday's distance run.*	OFF or 15–60 min. walking *Enjoy your last all-walking workout. This recovery session helps your muscles heal from the week by bringing them increased blood flow.*	*By this point, you probably want to run more. Be patient. Remember: It isn't about where you are today, it's about where you'll be by the end of this schedule. Also, if you can't finish 10 reps on Friday, repeat this week until you can.*

>

	Sunday	Monday	Tuesday	Wednesday
WEEK 1	OFF	Distance run: 20–25 min. *Start easy and build into your pace. Walk 5–10 min. first if it helps you warm up.*	OFF	Distance run + surges: 20–25 min., including 8 × 20 sec. surges, with 40 sec. jog recovery interval *"Surges" at this point are 20 sec. periods where you increase pace just a bit. Run at least 10 min. before beginning surges.*
WEEK 2	OFF	Tempo surges: 10 min. jogging warm-up, then 6–8 × 1 min. surges, with 1 min. slow jog recovery interval *Don't worry about an exact "tempo" pace—just run a bit faster than distance pace (breathing should increase), and jog a little slower for recovery intervals.*	OFF	Distance run + surges: 20–25 min., including 8 × 20 sec. surges, with 40 sec. jog recovery interval *Surges should be the same pace as Monday's surges or just a tiny bit faster.*
WEEK 3	OFF	Tempo surges: 10 min. jogging warm-up, then 6–8 × 2 min. surges, with 2 min. slow jog recovery interval *This workout will take a bit longer than previous Monday workouts. Be sure to include a warm-up: 10 min. easy running before first rep.*	OFF	Hill strides: 8 × 20 sec., with slow walk back to start line for recovery interval *Hill should be challenging, but not steep! Run with the same effort as surges last Wednesday. Walk slowly back down the hill after each rep. 10 min. easy running warm-up.*
WEEK 4	OFF	Tempo run: 5–10 min., with 10 min. easy running warm-up and 5 min. post-tempo jog *You're doing a single tempo rep today. Don't run harder than prescribed. Rasping breathing means you're running too fast.*	OFF	Short reps: 8–10 × 30 sec., 90% max effort, with 90 sec. walk/jog recovery *Today, you'll run a little faster, breathe a little harder. After each rep, walk 20–30 sec. then jog until the 90 sec. recovery is done. Quit if you're still breathing hard at 90 sec.*

Thursday	Friday	Saturday	Weekly thoughts
OFF	**Long run: 20–30 min.** *Your long run doesn't need to be any longer than your Mon. run this early in the schedule, and pace should be the same.*	**OFF or distance run: 20–25 min.** *If you're limiting yourself to 3 days per week, skip today. Otherwise, easy running.*	*For a beginner, this week is the most important of the entire schedule. Do it right, and you set yourself up well for the weeks to come. Overdo it, and you may face shin splints, Achilles tendinitis, or other issues.*
OFF	**Long run: 20–30 min.**	**OFF or distance run: 20–25 min.** *If you include an injury-prevention and resistance training routine (Key 14), this is a good day to schedule it—post-run, not before, and 1 set of easy-effort reps, no more.*	*Most of your improvement during the first weeks of training is due to nervous-system adaptations, not muscle adaptations. While it will take your muscles 4–6 weeks to really improve, your nervous system starts becoming more efficient on day one. So it's okay early on to set aside the 3-Week Rule (see Key 2) as you increase the intensity of your training. Your nervous system allows you to do more with the muscles you have.*
OFF	**Long run: 30–40 min.** *Because your legs are new to running, you'll increase your long run the week BEFORE introducing other increases in volume or intensity—a gradual introduction of increased stimulus.*	**OFF or distance run: 20–25 min.** *If you're doing the injury-prevention and resistance training routine, stick with 2 sets, but add some reps.*	*By now, you should be comfortable with 20–25 min. distance runs and rep sessions. If you feel you need a little more time at this level, repeat this week before moving on to Week 4 . . . because you're about to up your game.*
OFF	**OFF or distance run: 25–30 min.** *Long run moves to Sat. this week, and the length of your regular run increases. If you've been doing an injury-prevention routine on Sat., move it to Fri.*	**Long run: 30–40 min.**	*This week, you increase volume and intensity. Your Wed. workout introduces you to an interval workout (see Key 7), and you shift your long run to Sat. to recover from a harder Mon. and Wed. Don't run Mon.'s tempo as a time trial. It's a workout, not a race.*

>

	Sunday	Monday	Tuesday	Wednesday
WEEK 5	OFF	5K-pace reps: 8 × 1 min., with 2 min. recovery jog *You're back to 1 min. reps, but now they're faster. See weekly note for best way to establish correct pace.*	OFF	Hill run: 25–30 min. with 3–5 min. of uphill running *or* hill reps: 8 × 30 sec., with 60 sec. recovery walk/jog *Choices! Do a distance run with a bit of climbing or do reps on a challenging (not steep) hill. Choose the distance run if you have a long enough hill.*
WEEK 6	OFF	5K-pace reps: 6 × 2 min. with 3 min. recovery jog *Focus on pace for the first few reps. If you don't think you'll be able to finish the workout at that pace, slow down. If it's too slow, pick it up. You should finish with 1 rep left in the gas tank.*	OFF	Short reps: 8–15 × 30 sec., 90% max effort, with 90 sec. walk/jog recovery *This is a repeat of Week 4's workout except that the upper limit for reps has been raised. Only do more reps if your breathing has returned to normal at the end of your 90 sec. recovery.*
WEEK 7	OFF	Tempo run: 10 min. with 10 min. easy running warm-up and 5 min. post-tempo jog *Tempo is slower than the 5K-ish pace you've been running the past few weeks. Breathing should be elevated, but not rasping. You should finish your tempo feeling exhilarated, not exhausted.*	OFF or distance run: 30–40 min. *If you intend to run 5–7 days/ week, now is the time to add another distance day—these runs will contribute the most to your long-term fitness.*	Hill reps: 8 × 30 sec. with 60 sec. recovery *Hill should be challenging, but not steep. Use suggested warm-up from pp. 124–125. Walk the first 10–15 sec. of recovery, then jog slowly back to the start.*

Thursday	Friday	Saturday	Weekly thoughts
OFF	OFF or distance run: 25–30 min.	Long run: 30–40 min. *This was an intense week, so find a level-terrain course and take it easy. You need to recover.*	*This week, you'll do Mon. reps at 5K race pace. If you're not sure what that means, just wing it for now. Run hard enough to get your breathing going, but not so hard that you can't finish all the reps with energy to spare. On Wed., if you don't have access to hills, repeat the Week 4 Wed. workout.*
OFF	OFF or distance run: 25–30 min.	Long run: 45–50 min. *Length of long run increases this week. Focus on maintaining the same pace as in previous long runs.*	*As volume of reps rises (combined Mon. and Wed. workouts), the importance of a warm-up and cooldown also increases. Follow the guidelines (pp. 124–125) on warm-ups and slot in a 5 min. jog post-run to help your body recover from the workout.*
OFF	OFF or distance run: 30–40 min.	Long run: 45–50 min.	*Mon.'s 10 min. tempo begins to prepare you for the longer, sustained effort at an increased pace that defines the 5K, while the Tues. distance run allows you to increase volume significantly. The Tues. run also helps you to recover from the Mon. workout.*

>

	Sunday	Monday	Tuesday	Wednesday
WEEK 8	OFF	5K-pace reps: 4 × 3 min., with 3 min. jog recovery *The jump from 2 min. reps to 3 min. reps can be mentally tough. Expect it to feel hard, but also know that you're physically ready for this.*	OFF or distance run: 30–40 min.	Hill run: 25–30 min. with 5–10 min. uphill running *or* hill reps: 6 × 45 sec. with 2 min. recovery walk/jog *Same choice as in Week 5, but with more climbing in the hill run and longer reps for option 2. If you run reps, walk for the first 10–15 sec. of recovery, jog back to start, and wait there until 2 min. have passed.*
WEEK 9	OFF	5K-pace reps: 4 × 4 min. with 3 min. jog recovery *You'll do last Monday's workout but add 1 min. to each rep. Be sure to monitor pace so that you can finish all reps.*	OFF or distance run: 30–40 min.	Distance run + surges: 30–40 min. including 12 × 20 sec. surges, with 40 sec. easy jog recovery *Mon. was hard, so back off to short surges. Run faster than Monday's pace, but don't sprint—these should be fun, not fatiguing. Run at least 10 min. before surging.*
WEEK 10	OFF	Tempo reps (half-marathon tempo pace): 2 × 10 min. with 3 min. jog recovery *Tempo pace is slower than 5K pace. Don't try to match the pace you've run during Monday 5K-pace rep workouts!*	OFF or distance run: 30–50 min. *If you're feeling really good, stretch your regular distance run to 50 min. starting this week.*	Track workout: 8 × 200m, 5K/3K pace, with 200m slow jog recovery *or* short reps on the road: 10–15 × 30 sec. with 60 sec. walk/jog recovery (15 sec. walk/45 sec. jog) *Choices! Choose the track workout if you have a facility available. Start reps at 5K intensity, then try to pick them up for the second half of the workout.*

Thursday	Friday	Saturday	Weekly thoughts
OFF	OFF or distance run: 30–40 min.	**Long run: 45–50 min.** *This is your third week at 45–50 min. so if it feels easy, add some short climbs (no more than 3–5 min. total) to spice it up.*	*MILESTONE! The Mon. workout is your first VO₂max outing, where you surpass the magic 2 min. mark at which you reach VO₂max (Key 6). This means you'll start increasing the ability of your intermediate muscle fibers to create aerobic energy—the key ingredient of a faster 5K.*
OFF	OFF or distance run: 30–40 min.	**Long run: 50–60 min.** *Time to bump your long run up again. Add 3–5 min. of climbing if you'd like.*	*Mon.'s workout adds only 33% more time to the reps from last week, but it results in 200% as much work at near-VO₂max. Don't run too hard (finish with some gas left in the tank). You might find that this workout isn't any more stressful than 3 min. reps. That's your brain getting with the program (Key 13).*
OFF	OFF or distance run: 30–50 min.	**Long run: 50–60 min.**	*No hills this week. Your body needs to recover from Wed.'s track workout, and hills will interrupt that.*

>

	Sunday	Monday	Tuesday	Wednesday
WEEK 11	OFF	Track workout: 10–12 × 400m at 5K pace, with 200m jog recovery *This is a pace-work day. Run each 400m at what you feel will be your 5K pace. Jog a slow 200m between reps. Use the competition warm-up on pp. 124–125.*	OFF or distance run: 30–50 min.	Tempo run (half-marathon tempo pace): 10 min. with 10 min. easy running warm-up *Yes—a midweek tempo run! This is a good low-key follow-up to Mon. Don't turn it into a time trial.*
WEEK 12	OFF	Track workout: 6 × 400m, 5K pace, with 200m jog recovery *Same as last week, only quit after 6 reps. The idea is to solidify the pace (a nervous system adaptation) without fatiguing the body.*	OFF or distance run: 20–30 min.	Distance run + surges: 20–30 min. including 8–10 × 20 sec. surges, with 40 sec. jog recovery interval *Shoot for a pace that is just slightly faster than you expect to run on Sat.*

Note: Once you've completed this schedule, you can continue training by picking up at Week 5 or 6 in the 12-Week Plan, or by designing your own plan using the 12-Week Low-Intensity Plan (start anywhere in the plan).

During a surge, you pick up the pace to a prescribed intensity for a prescribed period of time.

Strides are 40–80m pick-ups.

Thursday	Friday	Saturday	Weekly thoughts
OFF	OFF or distance run: 30–50 min.	Distance run: 30–50 min. *With your 5K coming up in one week, shelve the long run for a normal-length run.*	*The Mon. workout before race week is your last hard training effort before the race. Use this workout to practice pace and improve fitness. Wed.'s workout reinforces the fitness gains you've made. Then it's time to dial it back and prepare your body to race.*
OFF	Easy distance: 20 min., plus younger runners do 4 × 60–80m strides at race pace	**5K RACE** *Focus. Have confidence. Run smart. Have fun!*	*Run your first 5K race! Some runners will choose to race before this point (use the 2-Week Adjustment on pp. 150–151), but it's not necessary at this stage of your development as a runner. You have a long journey ahead before you achieve your "best" 5K. Review Keys 22, 23, and 24, then relax and enjoy the race experience.*

2-Week Adjustment
for 5K Race (Beginners)

For beginners who choose to race before the 12th week.

	Sunday	Monday	Tuesday	Wednesday
RACE WEEK	OFF	5K-pace reps: 8 × 1 min. with 2 min. recovery jog	OFF or distance run: 50–75% of previous week's Tuesday run	Distance run + surges: 20–30 min. including 8–10 × 20 sec. surges, with 40 sec. jog recovery interval
POST-RACE WEEK	OFF	Distance run	OFF or distance run: same length as Tues. workout before race week	Tempo surges: 10 min. jogging warm-up, then 6–8 × 2 min. surge, with 2 min. slow jog recovery interval

Thursday	Friday	Saturday	Weekly thoughts
OFF	Easy distance: 20 min., plus younger runners do 4 × 60–80m strides at race pace	**5K RACE**	*If you choose to race before Week 12, be sure to taper in advance of the race. You'll also want to review Keys 22 and 23. Workouts this week reinforce intensity while lowering volume. And just because you're racing early doesn't mean you get a pass on racing smart. Review Key 24.*
OFF	OFF or distance run: same length as Fri. workout before race week	Long run: same length as last long run	*Prepare for some soreness. If you race before Week 12, you probably haven't fully prepared for the demands of a 5K. Sore or not, you'll want to schedule a moderate week. That means no hard Mon. workout and only tempo effort on Wed.*

12-Week Plan (plus 1 week base training)

This schedule applies to runners training 3–7 days/week, and does not include specified days for a post-run stretching and exercise routine or an injury-prevention and resistance training routine (Key 14). The former routine can be scheduled for any day of the week, though regular distance run days are advised. The latter routine should not be combined with a Mon. or Wed. hard workout.

	Sunday	Monday	Tuesday	Wednesday
BASE TRAINING ❙	OFF or distance run	Distance run, including 10 × 30 sec. surges, with 1 min. recovery jog *Do surges faster than distance pace, slower than 5K race pace. Run (easy) for 10–15 min. before starting surges.*	OFF or distance run	OFF or distance run
WEEK 1	OFF or distance run *If you're running 7 days a week, enjoy a distance run! If you're on a 3–6 days/week schedule, consider making this a day off.*	10K-pace reps: 8 × 1 min. with 1 min. jog recovery between reps *Don't push your first 2 weeks of Mon. workouts. Their purpose is to build muscle and connective tissue strength. Consider running them on the road and trail without keeping track of distance, just time (Key 6).*	OFF or distance run *If a Tues. run is on your schedule, it's a good day for a post-run stretching and exercise routine (Key 14).*	Short reps: 10–12 × 30 sec. at 3K pace, with 60 sec. recovery *This is a good workout to take to the road or trail, where there's less temptation to pick up the pace. Walk the first 10–15 sec. of your recovery, then jog.*
WEEK 2	OFF or distance run	5K-pace reps: 8 × 2 min. with 3 min. jog recovery *You'll pick up the pace a little from last week's reps, but don't overdo it, as you're still in a muscle and connective tissue-building phase. Use the full 3 min. recovery jog— your body needs it.*	OFF or distance run	Hill repeats: 8–10 × 30 sec., with 60–90 sec. recovery *If you don't have access to hills, use a treadmill or substitute short reps (Key 7). For recovery, walk the first 10–15 sec. then jog slowly back to the start.*

Runners who want to race before Week 10 can use the 2-Week Adjustment schedule on pp. 174–175, but it's highly recommended that you complete at least the first five weeks of this schedule before planning a race.

Thursday	Friday	Saturday	Weekly thoughts
Distance run + 6–8 × 60–80m strides, 85–90% max speed, with equal distance slow recovery jog *Do strides at the end of your distance run. Goal is to work your muscles while running a pace that's a little faster than what you'll run next week. Don't overdo it.*	OFF or distance run	Long run *Check the tables on pp. 126–127 for proper length (but consider going a little shorter your first time out).*	*The base training phase of this schedule is for runners who haven't been doing varied pace work. You'll need to give your faster muscle fibers a little work to avoid a case of DOMS in Week 1 of your actual schedule.*
OFF or distance run *If Thurs. is a running day for you, this is a good day for a post-run stretching and exercise routine.*	OFF or distance run	Long run (include 3–5 min. of uphill running) *A few minutes of hill work will strengthen your quads and hammies. Run the hill, don't race it. And take it easy on the downhill. If you don't have hills, a regular long run will suffice.*	*This week may look easy, but it's essential for strengthening muscles and connective tissue, improving stride by improving the nervous system, and increasing the pumping capacity of the heart—all of which will prepare you for the more challenging weeks ahead.*
OFF or distance run	OFF or distance run	Long run *Keep this run flat, even if Wed.'s workout put you in the mood for climbing. Your muscles need easy running—and you've got a hard workout coming on Mon.*	*Workout intensity increases this week, and next week too. This would seem to break the 3-Week Rule (Key 2). In reality, most of the initial gains you make in a training program are nervous system adaptations—you learn to do more with the muscles you have—so you can get away with these increases in intensity, as long as your volume remains relatively the same.*

>

	Sunday	Monday	Tuesday	Wednesday
WEEK 3	OFF or distance run	5K-pace reps: 6 × 3 min. with 3 min. jog recovery *If the jump from 2 min. to 3 min. reps seems too hard during your first reps, slow it down. A 5K pace is the goal, not an unbreakable rule.*	OFF or distance run	Hill repeats: 8 × 45 sec. with 2 min. recovery *For the 2 min. recovery, walk for the first 10–15 sec. then jog back to the start. If there's time remaining, walk or stand until next rep.*
WEEK 4	OFF or distance run	Tempo reps (half-marathon tempo pace): 2 × 10 min., with 2–3 min. jog recovery *Time to integrate a little tempo! Make sure to follow tempo-pace guidelines; if you run this at last week's 5K pace, you'll bonk big time.*	OFF or distance run	Short reps: 10–20 × 30 sec., 1500/mile or 3K pace, with 60 sec. recovery *If your legs feel strong, use 1500/mile effort. If you're fatigued, go 3K effort. Same recovery rules as during Week 1. Quit if you're still breathing hard after 60 seconds.*
WEEK 5	OFF or distance run	5K-pace reps: 4 × 4 min. with 3 min. jog between reps *With 4 min. intervals, half your reps are over the magic 2 min. mark. Maximize your training benefit with a full recovery between reps—if you need 4 min., take it.*	OFF or distance run	Hill repeats: 6 × 60 sec. with 3 min. recovery *For your 3 min. recovery, walk 10–15 sec., then jog back to the start. Walk or stand at the start for the remaining time—do not cut your recovery short.*
WEEK 6	OFF or distance run	Tempo reps (60-min. tempo pace): 4 × 5 min. with 2 min. jog recovery *Make sure to check the pace tables on p. 128, as you're running 60-min. tempo pace. If the tempo feels easy and your breathing is under control, 2 × 10 min. reps are okay (2–3 min. recovery).*	OFF or distance run	Hill repeats: 4 × 90 sec. with 5 min. recovery *90 sec. reps are a lot harder than 60 sec. reps. Expect some discomfort over the final 30 sec. For recovery, just jog back to the start, and then walk or stand until 5 min. have passed.*

Thursday	Friday	Saturday	Weekly thoughts
OFF or distance run	OFF or distance run	**Long run** *Today's long run is a good chance to go watchless. It's been a hard week, and your legs might appreciate the go-ahead to run easy (Key 4).*	*This week starts your attempt to rebuild your aerobic system bigger and stronger than it was before. Monday's VO$_2$max work takes you beyond the magic 2 min. mark (Key 6). And Wed.'s hill reps begin the process of turbocharging your mitochondria. You only get fitter from here on out.*
OFF or distance run	OFF or distance run	**Long run (include 5–10 min. of uphill running)** *Since you haven't run any hills yet this week, add some to your long run. Remember to just run the hills—don't race them.*	*If you're following the 3-Week Rule, it's time to increase your volume (overall mileage)— assuming you plan on increasing mileage (not all runners need to). Use the tables on pp. 126–127 to guide your increase. If you're running 3 days per week, limit increased volume to your long run (no junk miles tacked onto hard workouts).*
OFF or distance run	OFF or distance run	**Long run** *Flat terrain is probably best for today's run, but if you're feeling great, it's okay to include some climbing.*	*Many runners start feeling the urge to race after the first month, but I recommend that you wait another week. You need Monday's reps and some longer hill reps before toeing a line. See pp. 174–175 if you want to schedule a mid-program race.*
OFF or distance run	OFF or distance run	**Long run** *Last week it was okay to add hills to your run. This week, don't do it. Wed.'s reps were hard, and Mon.'s workout is a killer.*	*With workouts getting tougher, it's essential to include a post-run carb and protein snack. Your intermediate fibers are getting drained of glycogen in these workouts, and your muscles are taking a pounding. Nutrition is an easy way to boost recovery! (Key 16).*

>

		Sunday	Monday	Tuesday	Wednesday
WEEK 7		OFF or distance run	5K-pace reps: 5 × 4 min. with 3 min. jog recovery *This workout calls for 5 reps, but if you misjudge your pace and feel your tank running dry, skip the 5th rep.*	OFF or distance run	Track workout: 2 sets of 6 × 200m (first set at 5K pace, second set at 3K pace), with 200m jog recovery between reps, 3–4 min. break (can jog) between sets *This is a nervous system workout, not a muscle or energy-system workout. So don't skimp on the recovery—you need it to ensure proper nervous system adaptation.*
WEEK 8		OFF or distance run	Track workout: 12–16 × 400m, 5K pace, with easy 100m jog between reps *Run 400s at your current 5K pace—if you run them too fast, you'll bonk. Jog the recovery slowly. Also, if your 5K pace is slower than 25 min., see weekly note.*	OFF or distance run	Hill repeats: 6 × 90 sec. with 5 min. recovery *With six 90 sec. reps, it's important that you pace yourself correctly through the first reps. Run too hard, and you won't finish. Same recovery as Week 6.*
WEEK 9		OFF or distance run	Tempo reps (half-marathon tempo pace): 2 × 10 min. with 2–3 min. jog recovery *Step it back to half-marathon tempo pace this week, no faster. You're just reinforcing previous gains.*	OFF or distance run	Short reps: 10–15 × 30 sec., approx. mile/1500 pace, with 60 sec. recovery or track workout: 12 × 200m (3K pace), with 200m jog recovery *Faster, shorter reps with at least twice the time of the rep for recovery is the name of today's game. You're working leg speed for your upcoming race.*

Thursday	Friday	Saturday	Weekly thoughts
OFF or distance run	OFF or distance run	Long run (include 5–15 min. of uphill running) *This is a good week to add some climbing. But take inventory of how your legs feel after Wed. and only add as many minutes as you can safely handle.*	*This week's training is geared toward honing race speed and developing efficiency at goal pace. In Wed.'s workout, you'll use a watch and a specific distance to see where you stand. Don't panic if you're not quite where you want to be. You'll improve quickly over the next couple weeks. Also, if you're increasing volume, use the tables on pp. 126–127 to adjust run distances.*
OFF or distance run	OFF or distance run	Long run *No hills this week— no way.*	*This week, you transition from training for fitness to training for racing. Monday's workout helps establish stride efficiency at race pace. Wed.'s hills continue to turbocharge your new and bigger mitochondria. Note for Mon.: if you're currently 25 min. or slower for 5K, consider running 300m reps, with 100m recovery, instead of 400s—it's about time at pace, not distance.*
OFF or distance run	OFF or distance run	Distance run *With a tune-up race coming next week, it's a good idea to skip this week's long run— but it's not required. See weekly note.*	*With a race week coming up, a few of your workouts are geared toward that 5K. You'll work leg speed on Wed.—faster than race pace will make 5K pace feel easy. Also, cut your long run if you want to ensure your best performance at your tune-up race. But if you're feeling good (or have already run a race or two), you can keep the long run.*

>

157

	Sunday	Monday	Tuesday	Wednesday
WEEK 10	OFF or distance run	Track workout: 16–20 × 400m, 5K pace, with easy 100m jog between reps *This workout advances fitness for your Week 12 goal 5K. While it's too hard for a normal race-week workout, it's important to log this workout before your goal race.*	OFF or distance run	Hill repeats: 4 × 90 sec. with 5 min. recovery *4 reps is sufficient. This is part of a mini-taper for Saturday. Same 5 min. recovery plan as used previously.*
WEEK 11	OFF or distance run	Distance run *Saturday's race was a 100% effort—harder than any workout you've logged so far. You need extra recovery before another hard workout.*	OFF or distance run	Tempo reps (half-marathon tempo pace): 2 × 10 min., with 2–3 min. jog recovery *This workout helps reinforce positive adaptations in your slow-twitch and some intermediate fibers without overly stressing your body while you're still recovering.*
WEEK 12	OFF or distance run	5K-pace reps (road/trail): 4–6 × 3 min. with 3 min. jog recovery *or* track workout: 8–10 × 400m, 5K pace, with 200m jog between reps *Choices! I like 3 min. reps on the road, but you might prefer the track, where you can control the pace. If you choose track, note that recovery is 200m, not the normal 100m.*	OFF or distance run	Short reps: 8–10 × 20 sec., mile/1500 pace, with 40 sec. jog recovery, as part of 40–45 min. distance run *Run easy for at least 15 min. before starting reps. If your legs feel sluggish, add 2 reps up front at 3K–5K effort. This should not be a hard workout. You're just keeping your body in tune.*

Thursday	Friday	Saturday	Weekly thoughts
OFF or distance run (50–75% normal distance) *If your legs feel good, run 75% of your normal distance run. If fatigued, back off to 50% (even 40% is acceptable if you're really tired).*	OFF or easy distance for 20 min., plus younger runners finish with 4 × 60–100m strides, 3K effort *Following this workout, consider a session of rope stretching (Key 14).*	**TUNE-UP RACE OR TIME TRIAL** *(min. 3K, max. 5K)*	*Treat this tune-up race week as if it were goal race week. Review Keys 22, 23, and 24. Race smart—that way you'll benefit from a post-race assessment (Key 25). Don't worry if your time isn't what you were hoping for. You had a hard workout on Monday, and your brain needs a race or two before it will allow you a 100% performance.*
OFF or distance run *If you're running today, keep the pace easy. Your body is still recovering from and adapting to last Saturday's race.*	OFF or distance run *Same note as yesterday.*	Distance run *Just a normal distance run today—no long run. It's important to let your muscles, connective tissue, and nervous system fully recover for next week's race.*	*You may feel recovered by mid-to-late-week, but resist the urge to go farther or faster than scheduled. Most runners will benefit from a full week of recovery. If you're really chomping at the bit, change Wed.'s half-marathon-pace reps to 60-min. tempo-pace reps.*
OFF or distance run (40–75% normal distance) *For a mini-taper, cut today's distance to 75% of normal. Otherwise, do 40–50% of normal. Run easy, knowing there is nothing more you can do to improve for Saturday.*	OFF or easy distance for 20 min. plus 4 × 60–100m strides, 3K effort, for younger runners *Run easy. Resist the urge to "test" your legs—no overly fast strides, either. Older runners should skip the strides altogether. Consider adding post-run rope stretching (Key 14).*	**5K RACE** *Arrive early. Warm up. Race smart. Good luck!*	*Have confidence in your training and try to relax, even if you feel anxious or scared. Remember, once the race starts, you'll be fine. And if you race smart, you just might be shocked at how far your legs have come in the past 12 weeks!*

16-Week Extended Plan (plus 1 week

base training; running a minimum of 4 days per week)

This schedule applies to runners training 4–7 days/week, and does not include specified days for a post-run stretching and exercise routine or an injury-prevention and resistance training routine (Key 14). The former routine can be scheduled for any day of the week, though regular distance run days are advised. The latter routine should not be combined with a Mon. or Wed. hard workout.

	Sunday	Monday	Tuesday	Wednesday
BASE TRAINING 1	OFF or distance run	Distance run, including 10 × 30 sec. surges, with 1 min. recovery jog *Surges should be faster than distance pace, slower than 5K race pace. Run easy for 10–15 min. before starting surges.*	OFF or distance run	OFF or distance run
WEEK 1	OFF or distance run *If you're going to take a day off—and if Sunday is also a day off from work—then this is the day to do it. You'll either get a full day's break or a good opportunity to catch up on all those chores you've been postponing.*	10K-pace reps: 8 × 1 min. with 1 min. jog recovery between reps *First two Mon. workouts build muscle and connective tissue strength so that you can handle harder workouts later. See Key 6 on running these workouts on roads or trails.*	OFF or distance run *If you run, this is a good day for a post-run stretching and exercise routine (Key 14). Muscles are relaxed after an easy run, and mentally you won't be fatigued from a hard workout.*	Short reps: 10–12 × 30 sec. 3K pace, with 60 sec. walk/jog recovery *This workout is best run on roads or trails, where there's less temptation to run faster than required. Walk the first 10–15 sec. of your recovery, then jog.*

Runners who want to race before Week 13 can use the 2-Week Adjustment schedule on pp. 174–175, but it's recommended that you complete at least the first six weeks of this schedule before planning a race.

Thursday	Friday	Saturday	Weekly thoughts
Distance run + 6–8 × 60–80m strides, 85–90% max speed, with equal distance slow recovery jog *Do strides at the end of the run. Goal is to work your muscles while running a pace that's a little faster than what you'll run next week. Don't overdo it.*	Distance run	Long run *If you haven't been including a long run, it's time to start. See pp. 126–127 for proper length (but consider going a little shorter your first time out).*	*The base training phase of this schedule is for runners who haven't been doing varied pace work. You'll need to give your faster muscle fibers a little work to avoid DOMS in Week 1 of your training schedule.*
OFF or distance run *Another good day for a post-run stretching and exercise routine.*	Distance run *For 4-days-per-week runners, this is a good day to schedule an injury-prevention and resistance training routine—post-run, not before, and one set of easy-effort reps, no more.*	Long run (include 3–5 min. of uphill running) *Include a few min. of hill work to strengthen quads and hammies. Just run the hill, don't race it, and go easy on the downhill. If you don't have hills, a regular long run will suffice.*	*This 16-week plan includes more of the training that will guide you to your best 5K, but it also ups the risk of unforeseen variables (flu, work emergency, etc.) interrupting your schedule. A few missed workouts won't sabotage your program. If you miss more than that, repeat a week or use the keys in this book to get back on track. Stay confident and positive on your training journey!*

>

	Sunday	Monday	Tuesday	Wednesday
WEEK 2	OFF or distance run *If you haven't tried running without a watch, (Key 4), an easy Sunday run is a good time to experiment.*	5K-pace reps: 8 × 2 min. with 3 min. jog recovery *You'll go a bit faster and a bit longer today than last Mon., but you're still in a muscle and connective tissue strengthening phase.*	OFF or distance run	Technique drills: 1 rep of each drill from Key 15, plus 10–15 min. easy running post-drills *Jog back to the start after each rep, do an equal-length stride, and walk back to the start. If legs feel overwhelmed, do long skips and bounding. If drills are too much for you, just do easy distance and 8–10 strides.*
WEEK 3	OFF or distance run	Tempo reps (half-marathon tempo pace): 2 × 10 min. with 2–3 min. jog recovery *Half-marathon "tempo" pace means you are slowing down your pace from the last 2 weeks. Don't make the mistake of trying to match last week's pace. See Key 5 for a refresher on tempo.*	OFF or distance run	Short reps: 10–20 × 30 sec. 1500/mile or 3K pace, with 60 sec. recovery *If you're very fit, run this one at 1500/mile effort. If not, stick with a 3K effort. Remember, it's not about pace, it's about heart rate (Key 7).*
WEEK 4	OFF or distance run	5K-pace reps: 6 × 3 min. with 3 min. jog recovery *The jump from 2 min. to 3 min. reps can be a shock to the system. But the shock is mostly mental. Physically, each minute at 5K pace after the first 2 min. is more aerobic! See Key 6 for the explanation.*	OFF or distance run *Consider doing distance runs without a watch— the day after a hard workout, your legs are sometimes better off running even slower than the pace tables suggest. Let your body's feedback determine your pace.*	Technique drills: 1 rep of each drill from Key 15, plus 10–15 min. easy running post-drills *Do one rep of each drill. If you skipped bounding and long skipping last time, add them in today. But if you feel drills are too much for you, do easy distance and 8–10 strides.*

Thursday	Friday	Saturday	Weekly thoughts
OFF or distance run	**Distance run** *If you're doing the injury-prevention and resistance training routine, increase your volume to 2 sets of most exercises, 1 set of planks and—if you're sore—of Nordic curls.*	**Long run** *Avoid hills on your long run this week. Your muscles need to recover from Wed.'s drills.*	*In Week 2, you may be tempted to run a little harder during workouts than recommended, figuring you have plenty of time to recover if you overdo it. Don't. Never train harder than required to get the desired benefit. Your body changes and rebuilds incrementally. Try to speed up the process, and you don't get faster—you break in two.*
OFF or distance run	**Distance run** *For your injury-prevention and resistance training routine, it's okay to start increasing reps. See Key 14 for specifics.*	**Long run (include 5–10 min. of uphill running)** *Add a few minutes of hills to this week's long run. Run the hill but don't work it too hard. Breathing will naturally increase— you're fighting gravity—but if you're really huffing and puffing, slow down.*	*Tempo is fantastic for developing capillaries and mitochondria in all your slow-twitch fibers and about half your intermediate fibers. But you don't improve the workout by running harder than prescribed. The beauty of tempo is that you get most of the benefits of VO₂max workouts without taxing your nervous system or muscles nearly as much as you do with the latter workout.*
OFF or distance run	**Distance run, plus downhill strides: 4–6 × 15–30 sec., tempo effort** *Stick to recommended pace and length for downhill reps. Walk back to the start after each rep for recovery. Also shorten the distance run by a few miles. Slot the reps into the middle or end of the run.*	**Long run** *Take a little off the pace today. Your legs may be tender from yesterday's downhill reps. You need recovery.*	*Week 4 increases intensity and, if you're targeting higher mileage over the course of this schedule, volume. Use the tables on pp. 126–127 to figure your new regular and long distance runs—if you shorten Fri.'s run, spread the deleted distance over your other distance days. Stick to recommended intensity for all workouts. If you don't have hills for Friday's workout, stick with a distance run— don't substitute other reps.*

>

	Sunday	Monday	Tuesday	Wednesday
WEEK 5	OFF or distance run	Tempo reps (half-marathon tempo pace): 2 × 10 min. with 2–3 min. jog recovery *This run isn't just a good workout, it's also a nice respite from the heavy intensity of last week's training.*	OFF or distance run	Hill repeats: 8–10 × 30 sec., with 60–90 sec. recovery *For these short reps, pick your effort level depending on how your legs feel. Good—1500/mile effort. Tired—3K effort. For recovery, walk the first 10–15 sec., then jog slowly back to the start.*
WEEK 6	OFF or distance run	5K-pace reps: 4 × 4 min., with 3 min. jog between reps *With the increase from 3 min. to 4 min. reps, you double the amount of near-VO$_2$max work you get with each rep. For best results, jog the recovery interval—a faster pace recovery is counterproductive.*	OFF or distance run	Technique drills: 1 rep of each drill from Key 15, plus 10–15 min. easy running post-drills *If legs feel good, it's OK to try 2 reps of each drill (age 40+ runners stick with 1 rep). But add a minute more of recovery (standing is fine) between each set of 2 reps.*
WEEK 7	OFF or distance run *A good way to increase weekly mileage is to turn an "off" day into a running day—that way you can spread out the mileage.*	Tempo reps (half-marathon tempo pace): 1 × 20 min. *This is a continuous run—no reps or rest intervals. So be doubly careful to start at the right pace, as you won't have a break to rethink it.*	OFF or distance run	Hill repeats: 8 × 45 sec., with 2 min. recovery *For the recovery, walk for the first 10–15 sec., then jog back to the start line, and if you have time remaining, walk or stand until the next rep begins.*

Thursday	Friday	Saturday	Weekly thoughts
OFF or distance run	Distance run	Long run *It's okay to add 5–10 min. of climbing if you do this one on trails, but no steep hills.*	*After last week's increase in volume and intensity, you might be feeling a few aches and pains. Avoid ice baths, massage, or other stopgap procedures—they can aggravate a minor condition. Instead, allow your body to gradually recover over this less-intense week. If you haven't included injury-prevention and resistance training, now is a good time to start.*
OFF or distance run	Distance run, plus downhill strides: 6–8 × 15–30 sec., 10K effort *It's okay to pick up your downhill pace to 5K/10K effort, and to add a few reps. Shave down the length of your distance run and do the reps in the middle or end of the run.*	Long run *As with the last time your long run followed downhill reps—no hills this week!*	*As your Monday VO$_2$max reps get longer, it becomes even more important that you begin your workouts with sufficient muscle glycogen levels. It's imperative to include post-run carbs (minimum 200 calories), when your body replaces glycogen at an accelerated rate, and advisable to do the same with protein (20 grams). See Key 16.*
OFF or distance run	Distance run	Long run (include 10–15 min. of uphill running) *Increase your uphill minutes this week. Run the hills, don't race them. If you have no hills, consider some climbing minutes on a treadmill.*	*If you're following the 3-Week Rule—and if you're increasing volume—then its time to go back to pp. 126–127 and reset your runs. While this week is a step back in intensity, next week will turn up the dial again.*

>

	Sunday	Monday	Tuesday	Wednesday
WEEK 8	OFF or distance run	5K-pace reps: 5 × 4 min., with 3 min. jog recovery *If 5 × 4 min. is too difficult, stay with the 4 × 4 min. from your last VO₂max session.*	OFF or distance run	Technique drills: 1 rep of each drill from Key 15, plus 10–15 min. easy running post-drills *Younger runners have the option of doing 2 reps of each drill, as long as you add an extra min. to the recovery between each 2-rep set.*
WEEK 9	OFF or distance run	Tempo reps (60-min. tempo pace): 4 × 5 min. with 2 min. jog recovery *It's easy to turn 60-min. tempo-pace reps into 5K/10K-pace reps . . . don't, especially since you'll utilize a 2 min. jog recovery. If you find yourself running too fast, do a 3 min. recovery, then slow down for the next rep.*	OFF or distance run	Hill repeats: 6 × 60 sec., with 3 min. recovery *For your 3 min. recovery, walk for the first 10–15 sec. then jog back to the start. You'll have time remaining before your next rep, so either walk or stand until all 3 min. have elapsed.*
WEEK 10	OFF or distance run	5K-pace reps: 1 rep each of 3, 4, 5, 4, and 6 min., each with 3 min. jog recovery *This workout will result in 12 min. of near-VO₂max work—your toughest challenge yet.*	OFF or distance run	Hill repeats: 4 × 90 sec., with 5 min. recovery *For the recovery, jog back down the hill to the start, and walk for a minute or so. Then stand at the start line until the next rep.*

Thursday	Friday	Saturday	Weekly thoughts
OFF or distance run	Distance run plus downhill strides: 8–10 × 15–30 sec., 5K effort *This calls for 5K effort, but younger runners (under 40) can push that to 1500/mile effort if desired. Slot reps for the middle or end of the distance run. And walk back to the start line for recovery after reps.*	Long run *Keep it level post-downhill running.*	*Week 8 sees the end of technique drill sessions. If desired, you can add drills (1 rep each only!) as a warm-up to your Fri. distance run in Weeks 9 and 10, but don't do it if your legs are fatigued or if you have aches or sore spots.*
OFF or distance run	Distance run (optional technique drills) *If you want, add 1 rep of each technique drill (plus jog, stride, walk) as a warm-up to your distance run. Subtract the length of your warm-up and drills from the run.*	Long run *No hills if you did drills. Feel free to sneak in some climbing if you skipped the drills.*	*As this point in your schedule, you might be chomping at the bit to race. You will get more out of training at this point than racing, but racing can be irresistible. So feel free to schedule a race if you can't wait until Week 13—just make sure to follow the 2-Week Adjustment on pp. 174–175, then pick up this schedule where you left off.*
OFF or distance run	Distance run (optional technique drills) *Do 1 rep of each drill if you like, but be sure to subtract your warm-up and drills from the mileage covered during your distance.*	Long run *With the 90 sec. hill reps on Wed., it's best to keep hills out of your long run this week regardless of whether you did drills yesterday.*	*It's another 3-Week Rule bump week for volume. You'll maintain about the same intensity for 2 weeks as you did for the previous 3, which means you can afford to be a little more aggressive with your mileage. See pp. 126–127 to set your new distance run lengths.*

>

167

	Sunday	Monday	Tuesday	Wednesday
WEEK 11	OFF or distance run	Tempo reps (60-min. tempo pace): 2 × 10 min. with 3 min. jog recovery *Don't let your 60-min. tempo pace speed up to 5K or 10K pace. You should feel exhilarated, not exhausted, after the second rep.*	OFF or distance run	Track workout: 2 sets of 6 × 200m (first set at 5K pace, second set at 3K pace), with 200m jog recovery between reps, 3–4 min. break (can jog) between sets *This is a nervous system workout to prepare you for next Mon.'s workout. Do an easy 400m jog between sets, wait until 3–4 min. have passed, and you should feel faster on your second set.*
WEEK 12	OFF or distance run	Track workout: 12–16 × 400m, 5K pace, with easy 100m jog between reps *Run these at your current 5K pace. If that's goal pace, do it! But if you're not quite to goal fitness yet, don't fake it. Trust me, you'll bonk.*	OFF or distance run	Hill repeats: 6 × 90 sec., with 5 min. recovery *If your legs are beat up from Monday, substitute 20 min. of half-marathon tempo pace (any combination of reps) for today's hill reps. If you do the reps, same recovery as 2 weeks ago.*
WEEK 13	OFF or distance run	5K-pace reps (road/trail): 4–6 × 3 min., with 3 min. jog recovery *or* track workout: 8–10 × 400m, 5K pace, with 200m jog between reps *With a race on Sat., we cut back the volume of rep work (but not the intensity) for today's workout.*	OFF or distance run *For a traditional taper, cut this run to 50% of your normal-length distance run. If a traditional taper tends to leave you flat on race day, try a mini-taper (Key 21).*	Hill repeats: 4 × 90 sec., with 5 min. recovery *Because it's just a tune-up race on Sat., it's worth doing some hill reps today. Just don't do more than 4 reps, and perform the recovery the same as last week (or Week 10).*

Thursday	Friday	Saturday	Weekly thoughts
OFF or distance run	Distance run *Enjoy an easy-paced distance run. You need another down day, as next week includes a major bump in workout intensity.*	Long run (include 10–15 min. of uphill running) *Run, don't race, your hills.*	*This is your last week of pure VO₂max and aerobic strength training. From now on, you'll focus on goal pace and fine tuning your body for your fastest 5K. If you're dieting, now is a good time to wrap that up. You won't want to diet after this week, as you'll need your metabolism firing at full speed in order to run, race, recover, and supercompensate at your maximum level.*
OFF or distance run	Distance run, plus downhill tempo: 5–10 min. of downhill running, tempo effort *Don't exceed tempo effort here, as this will put an enormous eccentric load on your legs. Do the downhill tempo at any time during the second half of your distance run.*	Distance run *This is the week before a race, so cut your long run down to the length of a regular distance run.*	*For an intense week like this one—and because it precedes a race week—it's imperative to get the required recovery. Keep the carb and protein snacks coming post-workout. Make sure to get enough sleep. And don't overtrain during workouts, giving your body an exercise stimulus from which it cannot recover.*
OFF or distance run (50–75% normal distance) *Depending on whether you're doing a traditional taper or mini-taper (Key 21), cut 25–60% off the length of your normal run.*	Easy distance for 20 min.; younger runners can finish with 4 × 60–100m strides, 3K effort *Stick to easy running or jogging. Younger runners can do strides. All runners can benefit from a modified session of post-run rope stretching.*	**TUNE-UP RACE OR TIME TRIAL** *(min. 3K, max. 5K)* *Run this race with the same focus you'll apply to your goal race. Make sure to do a post-run assessment (Key 25).*	*Race week means race jitters! Review Keys 22–24 so that you don't succumb to the race-week mistakes that can sabotage training programs. If you start to get anxious, remember all the training you've done these past months. You've basically built a new running body for this outing—have fun taking it for a spin!*

>

	Sunday	Monday	Tuesday	Wednesday
WEEK 14	OFF or distance run	Distance run *No reps. Your tune-up race was a 100% effort, and it will require a longer period of recovery than the long run you'd normally log on Saturday.*	OFF or distance run	Tempo reps (half-marathon tempo pace): 2 × 10 min. with 2–3 min. jog recovery *By sticking to half-marathon tempo pace, you get a good workout for the muscle fibers that have recovered, but give your faster fibers and nervous system a little more time.*
WEEK 15	OFF or distance run	Track workout: 16–20 × 400m, 5K pace, with easy 100m jog between reps *Use your tune-up race to set the pace for these reps. If you find your rep times slowing down significantly (i.e., >5 seconds), it's time to quit the workout.*	OFF or distance run	Hill repeats: 6 × 90 sec., with 5 min. recovery *Only do the full 6 repeats if you also did 6 repeats for the Week 12 workout. If you've never done more than 4 × 90 sec., then repeat that today.*
WEEK 16	OFF or distance run	5K-pace reps (road/trail): 4–6 × 3 min. with 3 min. jog recovery *or* track workout: 8–10 × 400m, 5K pace, with 200m jog between reps *This is the same workout you did before your tune-up race. Again, you're trying to maintain intensity while cutting down on volume.*	OFF or distance run *Same taper rules as during your tune-up race pre-week.*	Short reps: 8–10 × 20 sec., 1500/mile (or 3K) pace, with 40 sec. jog recovery, as part of 40–45 min. distance run *This workout should be exhilarating, but not hard. If it feels hard, you're running too fast.*

Thursday	Friday	Saturday	Weekly thoughts
OFF or distance run	Distance run	**Long run (include 10–15 min. of uphill running)** *You should be recovered from your race, which makes it a good time to throw a little climbing into your long run. Keep the effort moderate, though, as you've got a big workout on Monday.*	*This is a recovery week. It's not just your muscles, connective tissue, and energy systems that took a beating in the race, it's also your nervous system. By allowing your body to recover and then supercompensate from the race, you'll find yourself more fit in the weeks to come.*
OFF or distance run	Distance run	**Distance run** *It's the week before a race, so cut down your long run to a regular-length distance run.*	*Monday's workout is your last chance to improve fitness before your Week 16 race. That's because it takes mitochondria 10–12 days to adapt. Big workouts too close to a race lead to reduced fitness, since mitochondria go offline until they've significantly adapted. FYI, if you were slower than 25 min. for your tune-up race, you can adjust Monday's workout to 16–20 × 300m, with the same 100m recovery—the workout is about time at 5K pace, not distance.*
OFF or distance run (40–75% normal distance) *Same taper rules as during your tune-up race pre-week.*	Easy distance for 20 min.; younger runners finish with 4 × 60–100m strides, 3K effort *Same guidelines as during your tune-up race pre-week.*	**5K RACE** *Have confidence in the training that brought you here. Trust in your ability to execute your race plan. Then do it.*	*Hopefully, your tune-up race week has prepared you for this week. You'll undoubtedly get anxious. Everyone does. Just don't use it as an excuse to make a mistake. Also, post-race, do an assessment, and decide if you want to try another 5K. If you do, simply repeat Weeks 14, 15, and 16, or use the 2-Week Adjustment schedule. For best results, race again within 3–4 weeks.*

12-Week Low-Intensity Plan

This plan is a framework for runners who want to create their own plan. Monday's workouts offer a standard, low-key progression of training designed to improve aerobic energy–producing capacity. You fill in the other days. Use the tables on pp. 126–127 to determine your distance runs. The post-run

	Sunday	Monday	Tuesday	
WEEK 1	OFF or distance run	10K-pace reps: 8 × 1 min., with 1 min. jog recovery between reps	OFF or distance run	
WEEK 2	OFF or distance run	5K-pace reps: 8 × 2 min., with 3 min. jog recovery	OFF or distance run	
WEEK 3	OFF or distance run	5K-pace reps: 6 × 3 min., with 3 min. jog recovery	OFF or distance run	
WEEK 4	OFF or distance run	Tempo reps (half-marathon tempo pace): 2 × 10 min., with 2–3 min. jog recovery	OFF or distance run	
WEEK 5	OFF or distance run	5K-pace reps: 4 × 4 min., with 3 min. jog between reps	OFF or distance run	
WEEK 6	OFF or distance run	Tempo reps (half-marathon tempo pace): 2 × 10 min., with 2–3 min. jog recovery	OFF or distance run	
WEEK 7	OFF or distance run	5K-pace reps: 5 × 4 min., with 3 min. jog recovery	OFF or distance run	
WEEK 8	OFF or distance run	Tempo reps (60-min. tempo pace): 4 × 5 min., with 2 min. jog recovery	OFF or distance run	
WEEK 9	OFF or distance run	5K-pace reps: 4 × 5 min., with 3–4 min. jog recovery	OFF or distance run	
WEEK 10	OFF or distance run	Tempo reps (60-min. tempo pace): 2 × 10 min., with 2–3 min. jog recovery	OFF or distance run	
WEEK 11	OFF or distance run	5K-pace reps: 4 × 5 min., with 3–4 min. jog recovery	OFF or distance run	
WEEK 12	OFF or distance run	Tempo reps (60-min. tempo pace): 2 × 10 min., with 2–3 min. jog recovery or 60-min. tempo-pace reps: 1 × 20 min.	OFF or distance run	

stretching and exercises routine and the injury-prevention and resistance training routine (Key 14) can be added on days of your choosing. Use the 2-Week Adjustment on pp. 174–175 when you're ready to race a 5K.

Wednesday	Thursday	Friday	Saturday
Option: Distance run; tempo run/reps; short reps; hill repeats	OFF or distance run	OFF or distance run	Long run
Option: Distance run; tempo run/reps; short reps; hill repeats	OFF or distance run	OFF or distance run	Long run
Option: Distance run; tempo run/reps; short reps; hill repeats	OFF or distance run	OFF or distance run	Long run
Option: Distance run; tempo run/reps; short reps; hill repeats	OFF or distance run	OFF or distance run	Long run
Option: Distance run; tempo run/reps; short reps; hill repeats	OFF or distance run	OFF or distance run	Long run
Option: Distance run; tempo run/reps; short reps; hill repeats	OFF or distance run	OFF or distance run	Long run
Option: Distance run; tempo run/reps; short reps; hill repeats	OFF or distance run	OFF or distance run	Long run
Option: Distance run; tempo run/reps; short reps; hill repeats	OFF or distance run	OFF or distance run	Long run
Option: Distance run; tempo run/reps; short reps; hill repeats	OFF or distance run	OFF or distance run	Long run
Option: Distance run; tempo run/reps; short reps; hill repeats	OFF or distance run	OFF or distance run	Long run
Option: Distance run; tempo run/reps; short reps; hill repeats	OFF or distance run	OFF or distance run	Long run
Option: Distance run; tempo run/reps; short reps; hill repeats	OFF or distance run	OFF or distance run	Long run

2-Week Adjustment for 5K Race

For runners who choose to race before the first scheduled 5K in their training plans.

	Sunday	Monday	Tuesday	
RACE WEEK	OFF or distance run	5K-pace reps (road/trail): 4–6 × 3 min., with 3 min. jog recovery *or* track workout: 8–10 × 400m, 5K pace, with 200m jog between reps	OFF or distance run	
POST-RACE WEEK	OFF or easy distance run	Easy distance run	OFF or distance run	

	Wednesday	Thursday	Friday	Saturday
	Short reps: 8–10 × 20 sec., 1500/mile (or 3K) pace, with 40 sec. jog recovery, as part of 40–45 min. distance run	OFF or distance run (40–75% normal distance)	OFF or easy distance for 20 min., plus 4 × 80–100m strides for younger runners (<40)	**5K RACE**
	Half-marathon tempo pace reps: 2 × 10 min., with 2–3 min. jog between reps	OFF or distance run	OFF or distance run	Long run

Acknowledgments

Toeing a 5K race start line, I feel utterly, nakedly alone. The gun goes off—or the horn sounds—and whatever happens next depends completely on me. If I go out too fast, I pay by the end. If my fitness isn't up to par, I pay no matter what I do. And even if things go perfectly, I have to deal with the pain of the last mile myself, forcing it aside in order to complete my race plan.

Thank goodness writing a book about the 5K is not like running one.

Here, I had an amazing team helping me every step of the way, correcting missteps and contributing ideas, edits, and the types of additions that make a book worth reading.

Before thanking individuals, I'd like to thank VeloPress, my publisher, for its faith in both me, as an author, and this book. Every writer dreams of having a committed and supportive publisher. I've got one. And I never take that for granted.

Next, I'd like to thank Casey Blaine, my editor, for suggesting this project and then applying her skill and commitment to mold it into final form. I'd also like to thank Sarah Gorecki, the project editor, and Christine Bucher, the manuscript's copyeditor. Big thanks to Vicki Hopewell, the book's creative director, for giving *Fast 5K* a look and feel that matches my passion for the race. Thanks also to Kara Mannix and Dave Trendler, marketing and sales, for their steady hand in navigating the path that lands this book in its intended audience's hands.

Finally, I'd like to thank every runner who's ever toed a 5K start line with me. One of my archrivals in masters (age 40-plus) competition once asked me why I kept writing articles that gave away my training secrets. I told him, "If you train incorrectly and slow down, you'll quit. If I help you to train better and race faster, you won't. I love this sport, and there's no sport without you. I'll do whatever it takes to keep you coming back." So thank you, fellow 5Kers, for our sport. I'll see you at the start line!

Index

About the Author

Pete Magill is the lead author of the book *Build Your Running Body*, author of *The Born Again Runner* and *SpeedRunner*, a former senior writer and columnist for *Running Times* magazine, and a current columnist for *PodiumRunner* magazine. As a 5K runner, Magill has the fastest-ever American times for age groups 45–49 (14:34.27 on the track), 50–54 (15:02 on the road), and 55–59 (15:42.13 on the track). He's a five-time USA Masters Cross Country  Runner of the Year, the fastest-ever 50-plus American for 10K (31:11), and a 2016 inductee into the USA Track & Field Masters Hall of Fame. He coaches for the Cal Coast Track Club, California Triathlon Club, and La Canada High School, and he's led his clubs to 19 national championships in cross-country and road racing. He lives in Pasadena, California, and competes for the Cal Coast Track Club.